Anouska Hempel

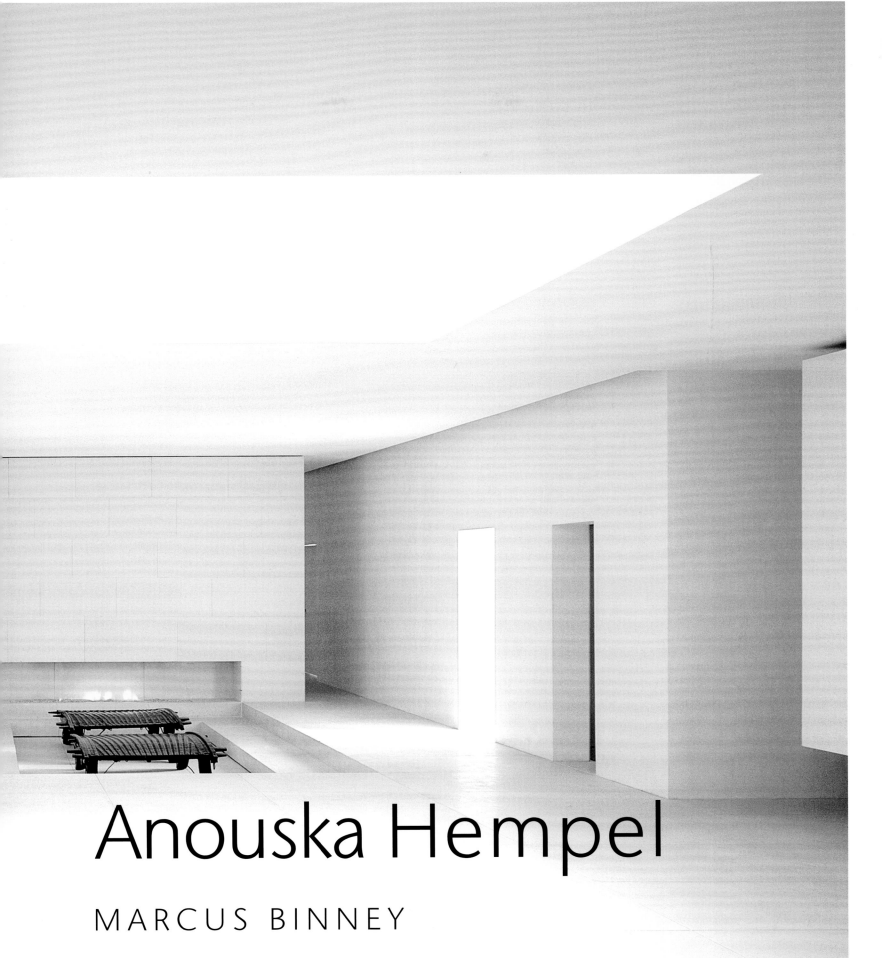

Anouska Hempel

MARCUS BINNEY

Cover: Long striped bed curtains settle on the floor like the train of a wedding dress, adding to the opulence of the room. Photo: Cameron Maynard/Aperto. Pages 2–3: The lobby of The Hempel is an essay in minimalism. Left: Anouska Hempel layers her interiors like an Old Master painter with a foreground, middle-ground and background, while reflections create subtle highlights. Opposite: The garden at Addison Road is a subtle palette of shades of green with leaves glistening after a fall of rain. Overleaf: At Addison Road Anouska Hempel strengthens the intensity of colour by limiting it to black and green. Note the perfect colour match between cushions and book jackets and the way the dried flowers echo the shape of the topiary outside.

First published in the United Kingdom in 2014 by
Thames & Hudson Ltd, 181A High Holborn, London WC1V 7QX

Reprinted 2022

Anouska Hempel © 2014 Anouska Hempel Design

Text © 2014 Marcus Binney
Essay © 2014 Belinda Harley

Designed and typeset in Cycles by Libanus Press

British Library Cataloguing-in-Publication Data
A catalogue record for this book is available from the British Library

ISBN 978-0-500-51769-7

Printed and bound in China by C&C Offset Printing Co. Ltd

FSC
www.fsc.org

MIX
Paper | Supporting responsible forestry
FSC® C008047

Be the first to know about our new releases, exclusive content and author events by visiting
thamesandhudson.com
thamesandhudsonusa.com
thamesandhudson.com.au

CONTENTS

INTRODUCTION

ANOUSKA HEMPEL COULD HAVE BEEN BORN IN ANY ERA, ANYWHERE IN the world, and however lowly or isolated, would have beaten a path to opportunity, success and good living. Central to her nature is a restless, adventurous spirit, a boundless ambition, a relentless drive imposed both on herself and everyone who works with her. Beauty and charm come in equal measure, mixed with a quick wit, remarkable repartee and a real power of fascination. These have led her to the temples of fashion and the salons frequented by money, power and taste. Never mind her incandescent temper, her impatience, her contempt towards those who cannot keep up with her or no longer amuse her, she has an untiring energy, an unquenchable appetite for work and for pastures new. The pace is maintained thanks to an astonishingly quick and perceptive eye that enables her to spot the intrinsic qualities of objects great and humble, and an acute sense of mood and atmosphere. She also has a phenomenally refined colour sense, the ability to match tones and shades, whether fabric, paints or hard surfaces, and to subtly grade or contrast them to enhance the richness and the layering.

With this comes an iron discipline, the desire and determination to control, to go on and on until every aspect of a room, a gown, a table arrangement or upholstery is done to her idea of absolute perfection. She achieves this not simply by giving commands and instructions, though there are plenty of these, but by a hands-on approach that will see her heaving furniture and sweeping floors as well as attending to the finest details of dress and jewelry. She can be both a princess and a trooper, with the vocabulary to match. Her work and that of her company, Anouska Hempel Design, encompasses interiors, furniture and furnishings, gardens, landscaping, food, hospitality in its widest sense and, of course, couture.

On offer is the total work of art, in German the *Gesamtkunstwerk*, a term used to describe the extraordinary creations of art nouveau architects and designers of the early 1900s. Architectural effects are one of Anouska Hempel's strengths. Her practice encompasses architecture in many forms – the design of buildings, sophisticated internal planning and the creation of strong architectural vocabularies, both modern and more traditional. Even when the work looks back it equally moves forward, creating novel, surprising and ravishing effects.

Hempel is self taught. She never attended a professional design course, or took an architecture or landscape degree. She has no diplomas in interior design or couture. Despite this, she is the archetypal professional, totally committed to her work, determined to refine and perfect, rejecting anything short of her ambitious goals.

She has had a major impact on many spheres of design, most notably hotels. At Blakes in London she invented the boutique hotel, where no room repeats another and a personal touch is everywhere apparent. What makes her work

Opposite: Black on grey – reflections in the indoor pool of a Salzburg home

Below: Full-length evening coat of black-figured satin with hoop-ringed hat in transparent fabric

Opposite: Rooftop pool in Majorca. Bold green and white stripes alternate with plain fabric to create a chic outdoor livery

so strong is her eye and feel for colour, for powerful, vivid colour, used to still more brilliant effect by carefully judged lighting. Her use of colour is all the more intense because so often it is a single colour, in several harmonious tones, combined with black or white, or shades of grey, to set it off.

With Anouska Hempel comes an incessant search for perfection and a determination to reject, refine, polish and tweak until it is obtained. Her opus is the result of teamwork. She works with both designers in her studio and with craftsmen, cabinetmakers, upholsterers and seamstresses who make her furniture, interior fittings, curtains and cushions.

Despite her well-known tempestuousness, those who work with her pay tribute to her talent and remain fiercely loyal. Most have stayed with her for years. The architect William Bertram explains, 'She is so fast that it is sometimes hard to keep up. She is the most inspirational person I know. I loved and adored her.' He continues, 'She will insist on moving walls, pushing or pulling them in and out to achieve a perfect floor. No cutting of tiles is tolerated. Her method is to begin with the floor.' He was so concerned by the knock-on effect of these changes at Cole Park in Wiltshire that he decided to provide plumbing in every room so that it would be available whenever remodelling required.

Her personal design process is not the traditional one of drawing with pen or pencil on paper. Instead it can be compared with that of Richard Rogers or Frank Gehry, whose designs evolve through numerous iterations. Her presentation brochures are almost entirely pictorial. However, although there is little writing, she herself is exceptionally articulate and vivid in her descriptions of concepts and designs. She is charming, expressive, a fount of witticisms and catchphrases. She is also freely critical of her own work as it develops. Her couture, with its superb command of elegant line, begins with a sketch of one half of a gown – in silhouette, leaving the maker to complete the pattern.

Below: A scarlet and shocking-pink strapless evening gown with full skirt forming a train and a scarf in matching silk. Below centre: Velvet and silk cushions add accents to the intense colours of the walls and curtains. Below right: A characteristic play on contrasting stripes

In the Salzburg house shades of grey and black are enlivened by sun, shadows and reflections

A few intriguing brushes in decanters

Line, whether straight or sinuous, is an important aspect of her work. She will demand that a box hedge is as level as a table. She also plays a subtle game of contrasts in which the perfect geometry of squares and oblongs – orthogonal design as it is called – is set off by the controlled use of softer forms such as cushions and upholstery.

In her interiors the convergence of lines often has the feeling of a Renaissance exercise in perspective, with the vanishing point at the end of the room or beyond. With this comes a sure and confident sense of proportion. It may be a variation of the traditional golden ratio, where one side of a rectangle is always more than half the length of the other to a proportion of 1.618. She also makes frequent dramatic use of exaggerated and attenuated forms – very long or thin – whether with her slender bamboo pole lampshades, or shelves and table tops with pronounced overhangs.

Scale, and the ability to master it, is crucial. Some architects cannot handle either very large or very small buildings. Hempel is capable of creating intimacy and intense privacy while also working in what may be called the Grand Manner. She sets out to both stun the eye and delight it.

The Grand Manner, in the French sense, is about creating imposing sequences of spaces – and also commanding designs that can be taken in at a single glance. The style was conceived by the 17th-century landscape architect André Le Nôtre

for the gardens of the Château de Vaux le Vicomte, but it applies equally to interiors. Central to the Grand Manner is the axis, a straight central line forming a vista around which every element extends in perfect symmetry, either real or apparent. But this is a game with many variants in which degrees of concealment can add further surprise, delight and incident as you move forward.

In Hempel's work the Grand Manner is enriched by the concept of layering and an Orient-inspired love of veiled effects, in particular the use of screens to add an air of mystery, partially concealing, but also hinting at what lies beyond.

Another element is the introduction of diagonal views as well as axial ones. Think of a plantation of trees in the form of a quincunx – each trunk on a perfect grid. Wherever you stand, you look along a precisely formed avenue, both ahead and to the sides. In addition, the trees line up diagonally to create further intriguing vistas. At Blakes London, with its voluptuous use of fabrics, the diagonal views across four-poster beds to windows with matching hangings are captivating. Here, too, as in so much of Hempel's work, the frame is as important as the picture – often consisting of swagged and gathered fabric.

One of the most dramatic forms of framing is the enfilade – a military term indicating a straight, clear firing line. In interiors it describes a series of doors in perfect alignment and all matching in size to give the effect of breathtaking length and absolute order. It evolved par excellence in the design of palaces and

Sun and shadow create patterns in the all-green palette of hedges, lawns and trees at Cole Park. An Anouska Hempel garden can have as much precise geometry as any room

The same precision applied to napkins

Framed panels of wax seals show how symmetrical groupings add appeal to objects of every kind

Below: Reflected in a mirror, cushions resemble a colony of penguins. Below right: More horizontally stacked cushions and angled stripes play visual tricks

grand houses where the intention was to dazzle as well as to delight. Hempel employs enfilades repeatedly both in hotels and houses.

Traditionally an enfilade is created by aligning a series of connecting doors between rooms. Usually these are doors set close to the windows so that the view is complemented by sunlight streaming in to create repeating patterns on the floors. Hempel adopted enfilades to masterly effect in the Grosvenor House Apartments on Park Lane, London, where spaces are connected by doorways without doors.

These apartments manifest another element of her work – the use of groupings to produce special effects. Almost any object or piece of furniture can be made more striking if it is one of a pair, and in Hempel's interiors lamps, tables and mirrors are regularly paired to increase impact. Objects are also clustered in threes, fours and sixes, and at times tens or a dozen. In particular, framed prints – often architectural ones – are double- or triple-banked and hung in fours or sixes. At Cole Park, bird's-eye views of country houses are hung beneath windows as well as beside them. At the Grosvenor House Apartments, sets of framed mirrors little more than a foot square are arranged in eights or tens as in the panels of a door. For added effect the frames are boldly modelled to resemble the black ebony frames used for Dutch Old Masters in 18th-century picture cabinets. 'I tell my team, "If you like something enough to buy one, buy the lot. You'll never see them again,"' Hempel says.

Every tabletop offers up a still life or tableau, with arrangements of lamps and candles, themselves of geometric shapes – cubes and spheres – or apples and pears. She takes a similar approach to table laying. On the Turkish gulet *Beluga*, each placement is a stepped pyramid, its tiers of plates made from stitched leather as well as tin from Turkey, pewter from Italy and marble from India.

A sense of mystery is created by the clever use of reflections. Architects and designers have long been fascinated by the Soane Museum in Lincoln's Inn Fields, London, where the Regency architect Sir John Soane placed slivers of mirrors to reflect light into dark passages and corners, creating spaces that existed only in the eye of the onlooker. Hempel, too, makes skilful use of mirrors and reflections, and has designed her own form of movable screen mirror to create similar artful effects. It comes in a tall gilt frame with a baroque scallop top, and can be set singly or hinged in twos, threes and fours, and then positioned to reflect light and vistas from different angles – there are examples in the dining room at Cole Park.

Evening light is as carefully considered as daylight. The entrance hall at Cole Park, with candles lighting all the windows upstairs as well as downstairs, is as magical a sight as the Château de Vaux le Vicomte when lit for evening openings in midsummer. In Hempel's interiors, evening light is usually softened and the source concealed – dark lampshades throw out pools of light below and above. Dozens of candles are grouped together to add warmth and lustre animated by a live flame. Shadow is as important as light and it is the play of the two that creates the magic. For other interiors, she makes use of strong directional lighting, using ceiling spots to focus intense light on glowing colour, as for example on the sumptuous fabrics in the Cardinal Suite at Blakes in London.

Growing up in the bright light of the southern hemisphere, Hempel has always found the grey skies of England a challenge. Her response has been to systematically shut them out from the windows of her houses. She does this by filling her gardens with greenery, mainly evergreen shrubs and trees – clipped balls of laurel, box, ivy and yew – which retain an intense colour all year. Inside, the window blinds are often pulled down to conceal the upper panes and any glimpse of dull sky that might emerge between the trees and topiary.

The range of Hempel's work is significant in its geographical extent. Her practice has extended to every continent except her own, Australasia. It is found in the world's great capitals and in most cosmopolitan and fashion-conscious cities – Istanbul, Milan and New York, as well as London and Paris. Her sense of romance has brought her commissions on islands and great lakes: on Java, Majorca and Singapore – as near an island as a peninsula can come – on the shore of Lake Lugano and in the mountains of Salzburg and Vaduz. She is currently working in the Persian Gulf, Lebanon, Morocco, Chile and Brazil.

Equally impressive is her long association with the world's leading brands – Van Cleef & Arpels and Louis Vuitton – as well as individual fashion houses such as Henry Cotton's in Milan. Inevitably, many of these interiors have changed and been remodelled since, but at Saint-Germain-des-Prés in Paris, Louis Vuitton – a firm with an exceptional sense of its history and ancestry – has maintained her 1980s store with pride and meticulous care.

Hempel's interiors may be compared with those of other periods renowned for their total effects, such as rococo and art deco. Adolf Loos, the Austrian Secession architect, tells the story of a rich man whose house an architect had designed down to the finest detail, down even to the placement of his bedroom

A simple vista animated by intriguing shapes

A dark, even mysterious, palette is brought alive by flashes of white against a dark slate floor

ANOUSKA HEMPEL

slippers. The house soon became unbearable as a result. All-enveloping decorative schemes can be suffocating – a fact that partly explains the disappearance of so many art nouveau interiors within a decade or two. A similar fate met the highly decorative rooms of Jacobean England whose trompe l'oeils imitating panelling, fabric and tapestries rarely lasted more than thirty years because they frayed and the owners could not cope with the stage-set richness any longer.

Anouska Hempel overcomes these risks in three ways. Firstly, although her interiors have all-encompassing decorative schemes, they all come with a manual explaining in precise detail how they can be maintained in a pristine state. Secondly, her designs usually include a personal play on the wedding refrain of something old, something new, something borrowed. These elements might be the brilliant packaging she adores – the red coffee tins, the hat boxes, the canvas luggage – enamel vases, prints of flowers and architecture, or, as at the Grosvenor House Apartments, sepia photographs of new London landmarks. But, almost always, there is also a feature that has been commissioned, designed and made for the room, as were, for example, the intriguing Thai cheese graters on the cabin doors of her gulet, *Beluga*. Chinese horoscope wheels, Regency hound's head snuff boxes, Ethiopian ceramics, 17th-century Italian prints, Victorian ostrich-feather fans, Japanese garden benches and lacquered pillows are all among the thousands of exotic items that have caught her eye and brighten her interiors.

Thirdly, Hempel has the ability to transform and reinvigorate her own work. Cole Park has been revitalized and enriched in successive makeovers, which leading photographers have documented for various magazine articles. Here, the interiors began quite simply but over time every surface became home to a perfect still life of carefully composed objects. An alert and lively eye will home in on any small object with some intrinsic value. It may be expensive or everyday and cheap, but she is able to see instantly how it should be displayed and grouped to good effect. This marriage of shapes and forms delights and amuses – wit is an important element of her design and her clever compositions have the ability to draw a smile or an exclamation of delight.

Fundamental to Anouska Hempel's work throughout her career has been a strong streak of romance: 'Romantic places? I live in them all the time. Anywhere the trade routes have passed or the trade winds have blown – that's my territory. I can dream myself into a desert tent playing footsie with Genghis Khan, or a military tent planning strategy with Napoleon. Wherever my imagination finds itself that's where my rooms begin.' She explains: 'I always have fires in both summer and winter. It's about romance.' If a choice has to be made between style and comfort, style wins every time.

Opposite: Layered curtains frame not just the bed but the vista beyond

Overleaf: In a house at Salzburg, in the half-light of dawn, sunrise brings a momentary flash of intense colour while the house and the trees outside remain monochrome

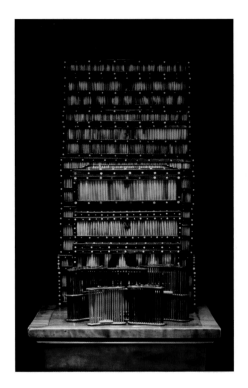

A stack of bamboo trunks, each fractionally smaller than the one beneath

Exotic, richly wrought oriental furniture, often bought while travelling, has a special appeal for Hempel

ANOUSKA HEMPEL IS A SAVANT OF THE VISUAL – A DESIGNER WHO SEES everything and understands it instinctively. This is not an academic process: were she to come across a Zen temple, for example, or a Tudor portrait, she will grasp its aesthetic significance immediately, without having had the background or previous experience to do so. She sees what it does, *and how it does it*, and proceeds straight away to use the language of its art as if she had spoken it since childhood. She can take a source of inspiration, understand its disciplines and then use it with brio, transforming it in entirely original ways. It is this creative friction that produces sparks and marks out each design as unmistakably her own.

It is axiomatic that designers must extend themselves: the painter who experiments with ceramics; the fashion designer who launches a line of tableware – each a calculated progression. But Anouska Hempel is not one of these. What is remarkable about her career (and by extension her influence as a designer) is that she sees everything, as of right, as her domain: at its heart, interior design and architecture; but also couture, garden design, original food and recipes, glassware, pens, beauty products, millinery, floristry, topiary. Each is an element in a complete life design.

Her sources of inspiration act as creative stimuli; nothing is simply copied or used as it is. For example, the impact of a single red and white calligraphic figure, stamped on to a piece of wood in a market in Japan, can ignite her imagination. The image resurfaces, transformed, as a swagger of ochre against parchment in her couture; in an exuberant red Chinese room at Blakes in London; and in a detail on a table. Objects, styles, colours and symbols from different cultures all act as catalysts.

MASCULINITY

One of Anouska Hempel's key sources of inspiration is the massive, austere Zen temple at Nanzen-ji, in Kyoto – it forms a mighty touchstone for her artistically. The temple's vast structure of pillars with iron bands and columns opening up into a monolithic, dark roof space, is uncompromisingly masculine. To some this might seem forbidding, but to Anouska Hempel it is a challenge: 'It is monumental and confident. It is my business to keep faith with that confidence and transport it, to take it with me, to wherever I am going. . .'

All of her work shares this direct, masculine quality: it is bold and unafraid. This is true whether she is designing a restaurant, a gown or a garden. Most notably, it is manifest in the driven strength of her architectural work at the minimalist Hempel hotel and in her new resort at Warapuru in Brazil, where she handles monolithic forms with assertive ease. In many respects, she is not a 'feminine' designer at all, and her interiors, though they may be detailed, are strong and invigorating rather than soft. Nowhere in her work is there anything 'sweet'.

CONTROL and SYMMETRY

Anouska Hempel's work is all about control: achieving it or being in mischievous conversation with it. When she saw tea bushes in a Kyoto plantation, long snaking green rivers of perfectly clipped cultivation, they came to encapsulate what she strives for: 'This is *important*. They exercise such great control. The way the roots are clipped, the way the shapes are formed, the way the crop is cut – absolutely everything was magical to me. The way the women rolled down the nets precisely, the way they employed fans to ensure that the mist and frost were kept off: it was total control. The rhythm and the magic of that, which occurs all over Japan, has influenced me enormously.'

Control and symmetry characterize her work: in the detail of a jacket in her couture; in objects placed with military precision at exactly 90 degrees to a border; on a large scale in landscapes; and as minutiae to delight one on a bedside table. It does not matter that this order may be transitory: it is always worth striving for. She was enchanted by the sight of how fish in a Japanese market had been arranged, with perfect symmetry, on a block of melting ice.

The reverse of this, of course, is the wild and the asymmetrical. As Anouska Hempel remarked of the tea plantation, where they could, they controlled everything, 'and when they knew they couldn't control it, they let it go wild. I can do it myself, this control and symmetry, in short bursts; but the continuity breaks down because it is something very hard to keep up in this day and age and I am in the service business.' People take what she creates, compromise its strict aesthetic and change it – but the guidance, if they choose to follow it, is there: each house or interior completed by Anouska Hempel comes with a manual, describing everything from the display of dishes to the arrangement of towels and linen. Each aspect of living in the house and maintaining it is covered in detail. Anyone believing that this is merely the sign of an addiction to control is missing the point: details are terribly important – there is a best place to put a table light, a mirror or an object *because it contributes to the whole*.

Anouska Hempel's view of the world has much in common with the Elizabethans' understanding of a world order that follows the ordered movement of the heavens – a dance to the music of the spheres. She has an almost physical abhorrence of things that look, and are, slapdash: 'I am not really mad about "anything goes"; I like it in conversation, in characters – but not otherwise.'

WATER

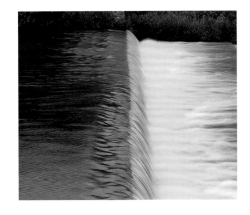

By contrast, water, with its sheer unpredictability and autonomy, appears throughout her work. The Japanese use of water as a living feature has influenced her profoundly: 'Seemingly everything in Japan is surrounded by water. It is how you use the water, how you set yourself in the water, it's what you do with it – every culture has a different take.' In her design for a house in Salzburg, she employed water as a frame with unsurpassed brilliance and severity. At the house in Addison Road, London, surfaces are given the character of water – witness a marble floor, reflecting dark green like a deep, still pool.

JUXTAPOSITIONS

Anouska Hempel is ultra-sensitive to juxtapositions. 'Everything to do with the juxtaposition of textures is terribly important to me: the rough with the smooth.' She also loves the juxtaposition of the great and the small, the heavy and the fragile. She is exhilarated by the way that the great strength manifest in Japanese architecture is set always against the flimsy, fragile, 'yet so uncompromising' Japanese way of living. The monolithic strength of a temple roof versus paper-thin screens and delicate origami; the strong, severe aesthetic of a Japanese garden and the exquisitely vulnerable petals of cherry blossom.

BORDERS, BANDS and PERIMETERS

It was said of the artist Patrick Caulfield that he painted within precise black lines because, paradoxically, he was such a free artist that he imposed the discipline of lines upon himself, as a structure for his art to inhabit. So Anouska Hempel, too, is an artist of borders, bands and perimeters. Her inspiration, once again, is especially evident in Japan, where bands of heavy granite beside gravel, finely raked, provide structure. 'This gives strength and texture, which leads you somewhere. I do my perimeters very carefully and very strongly, and wherever we are working, on great buildings or on small details, every single stone has a definite imperative. There is a reason why it has been laid there if you want to look into it.' At Cole Park in Wiltshire she has produced perfect examples of this in the gardens. The garden at The Hempel was designed as a small masterpiece of borders and textures in controlled bands. Look about you and you will see that this theme runs like an insistent heartbeat through everything she does.

EMBOSSING and FRETWORK

Embossing and fretwork are important visual prompts for Anouska Hempel. Embossing is a passion: a crest will be repeated in soaps, in exquisite raised embroidery on linen, and on walls. A water conduit from Japan is one example of how fretwork can inspire her. 'Fretwork, which is associated completely with the French in my mind, is nonetheless there in Japan, done all those thousands of years ago – here is something exquisite that was just used for a drain to let the water flow downhill.'

RED

The artist Paul Klee wrote that 'all art is a memory of age-old things, dark things, whose fragments live on in the artist'. We can see this process at work in Anouska Hempel's practice. When she first saw a powerful piece of calligraphy, she said, 'That image will stay in my mind, to work as an existential pattern, perhaps first somewhere in someone's house and it will go galloping on to some greatness somewhere, because it has got me.' Part of the impact of the image lay in its use of red, a colour that is a dominant force in her world-view: 'Red to me is a very strong, heavy colour – a dominating colour, which I love to use in England, as I feel that in the grey of English days, red and warmth are very important . . . .

I will use red flowers in a bowl on a dark wood table. If red is used subtly, it can be used very well.' Downstairs at Blakes in London, oriental interiors glow ochre; in Blakes Amsterdam, the muted grey light of the Dutch canals is warmed by the turmeric, flame colours of the Spice Route; in her couture, red is sexy, powerful and elemental. That one piece of red and white calligraphy, she explains, 'inspired ridiculous things like a red grosgrain ribbon on a white chalky pole.'

VISUAL GAMES

Trompe l'oeil is one of Anouska Hempel's particular signatures. She uses it triumphantly: in blue and white, as a cleverly repeated copy of Delft tiles; to add drama in the Corfu Suite at Blakes; and especially at Cole Park, where it features with great *esprit* as a lion's head that appears on floors and along walls. Throughout her work, it is employed for 'making excuses, winding up this and that, covering walls, taking a tapestry around a corner . . . for wit and mischief'.

LAYERING

What does Anouska Hempel do with all these different sources of visual inspiration? The answer is something she calls *layering*, which is fundamental to her work as a designer. It is, for her, the process of laying, overlapping or stacking things of different dimensions, object upon object, culture upon culture, over or on top of one another. 'Vertical or horizontal, colour on colour, mass on mass, boldness against softness. It is the layering of one's imaginative life on a decorative level: you have to add to it every month or two, or year or two; you have to find yet another thing which will work with that particular table . . . . The client needs to understand that this doesn't just happen out of the blue, finished. You don't just buy the curtains and the table and then it all "happens". It is a matter of magic and mystery, a process that takes place after you have created the bones. That is something you have got to get across to people: that you must keep on going. Don't just think "I have done that." Never, never stop.'

THAILAND and COLOUR

When Anouska Hempel left Australia, with its wide empty spaces, arid, harsh climate and earth scorched from bush fires, and arrived in Thailand, it was to be immersed in colour for the first time in her life – a civilization of colour, of shots of hot pink and silver amid impossibly lush green. 'I am enormously influenced by little things. In my early days in Thailand, I was deeply influenced by the astonishing costumes in the mountains in northern Thailand, especially among the Meo, Lisu and Akha peoples. A child's hat with intense pink pompoms illustrated a whole way of life by the strength of the colour. These little things infuse themselves into my work, especially into the couture; they all get mixed up together and land up somewhere – either on a cushion, on a stripe or on someone's head; on a dress. . .something happens! I was like a sponge taking the whole thing in – the smells, the sensitivity.' Collecting costumes from the Golden Triangle of Southeast Asia became important to her: her collection has

been on show, and applauded, in Blakes London ever since. 'Everything to do with Thailand has a meaning for me. Because of the opium growing, and the dangers of thieving, they sewed everything they owned onto themselves. You never hung anything up on the wall – every single piece of your wealth was hung on you, from your head to your toes.'

THE ELIZABETHANS

In many rooms designed by Anouska Hempel you will find looking down upon you from across the centuries the grave, precise beauty of a Tudor portrait. They figure so widely in her interiors that they are a leitmotif – and sometimes the source of inspiration for the room itself. She began collecting early Elizabethan art as soon as she could, a pioneer in a field that is now much followed.

A specific colour, or a couple of colours, in a portrait could set the palette for an entire room, as with her exquisitely fashioned dining room at Addison Road, London. An Elizabethan portrait of rich, old gold and varieties of black set the tone for this concoction of black and yellow – all Biedermeier furniture and black and yellow striped silk. When she bought it, the portrait had a mature colour from years of exposure to tobacco smoke, but she chose to leave it uncleaned; the distinctive colour of the patina it had acquired became her inspiration for the room.

Sometimes a detail from these portraits catches her inner eye: an intricate lace cuff may reappear in a completely different incarnation in her couture. The way that Elizabethan portraiture shows the individual emerging from the stylized also appeals to her. The Elizabethans gloried in personal display. Many of the women painted in dresses of extraordinarily ornate, bejeweled splendour, did not own this attire; the dress was the property of the travelling artist, who recognized his sitters' need for status through adornment.

Anouska Hempel also loves how the Elizabethans treated the female form. It was a time of stomachers and farthingales, which ensured women stood erect. In her own couture, she has taken this rigidity and given it a twist. In her dresses a woman's body is sculpted to look longer, leaner and yet still with strong curves. It is said of an Anouska Hempel ball gown that while its hidden corsetry does hold a woman upright, this makes her feel, not constrained, but relaxed, protected, safe.

SCREENS

English Regency, European, Japanese – Anouska Hempel is a collector of screens and a maker of screens, too. She likes to create filtered light; the illusion of a further dimension, of a half-glimpsed space, the mystery of a room beyond. 'What I do is use a screen, something very static and immobile, to create an illusion. I might also take a screen and hang it over a frame, so that you have movement, like the way they have of hanging things up in Japan: wired trays which move, rattle a bit, and have a bit of clatter to them.'

In the restaurant at Blakes in London, she glued black fretwork trays on to clear glass screens to deepen the perspective. The room feels larger as a result and, despite being in a basement, less restricted, giving diners an important sense of being partially enclosed and therefore intimate. In domestic interiors, she has her own craftsmen make up Japanese *sudare*, screens for the windows, to soften the hard grey English light. In Blakes Amsterdam, her use of screens is little short of masterful in a 17th-century house warmed by a colour scheme of saffron, turmeric and paprika, an evocation of the Dutch East India Company's Spice Route.

A Japanese parable, involving the 16th-century tea master Sen-no-Rikyu, tells of how he built a garden enclosed by a tall hedge that blocked the view of the sea. The client for whom the garden was built is unhappy with the result – until he bends over to rinse his hands in the water basin. Then the sea becomes visible in a gap between the hedges and the client smiles. As the tea master had hoped, the client realizes the intention behind the design: 'His mind made the connection between the water in the basin and the great ocean and thus between himself and the infinite universe.'

This is something Anouska Hempel creates, too – she has a fascination with screening off horizons in order to define and emphasize them. 'Screening and layering', she says, 'will always come up in my work.' At Cole Park she lined an avenue with white horse chestnut trees to frame a pin-point of distant horizon, to which you are drawn. In a minimalist work of landscaping at a house outside Salzburg, she planted serried lines of beech that hide, and then suddenly reveal, the mountains. Her watchword: 'Design, refine and repeat.'

EVERY STORY...BECOMES A PICTURE

On a visit to the pyramids in Egypt, Anouska Hempel was struck by a far-off light – a moving star, shining down a deep shaft. The atrium at The Hempel was her response to this. 'I wanted a light source above. In London, in the end, I improvised with a projector, because we could never find stars in a London sky.' She absolutely loves stories, and objects, for her, tell tales. For example, a collection of ivory cricket cages leads her to picture ladies of high rank in Imperial China as they listen to the crickets concealed in tiny, perforated cages – the size of little scent bottles – in their long sleeves. Bernardo Bertolucci's 1987 film *The Last Emperor* – in which the boy king is made to choose his first concubine based only on the silhouettes of girls dancing behind gossamer silk – inspired her to play a similar trick. The result: the dancing feet of waiters behind a 'floating wall' at The Hempel.

Beluga, the Turkish gulet Anouska Hempel transformed, is a floating myth, its black sails throwing darkness into the water at sunset, suggesting to all who see it tales of a thousand and one nights. Antique Louis Vuitton luggage and vintage trunks with beautiful locks and embossed corners feature as low tables on board the boat, and in the lobby at Blakes London, where they hint at journeys yet to be taken. There is clearly a process of storytelling here. *Beluga* is the realisation of romance and myth, conceived as if it were setting out to Phoenician ports, where men would talk of exotic perfumes, of spices, of quests for an Ithaca.

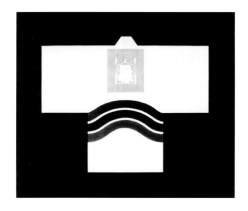

A PORTRAIT OF THE ARTIST

No study of Anouska Hempel would be complete without looking at her own role as an inspiration: it is tremendous. The first minimalist hotel – the first 'boutique' hotel, a term she does not like but a concept of brilliance – brought into being with Blakes in London; the presentation of food raised to an art (rather than a pretentious craft); the use of topiary, massed and distinctive, in landscapes, in town gardens, in borders, on terraces, on tables and in bedrooms . . . all these are Anouska Hempel's contributions.

Certain materials, like black slate on which food may be arranged, have become a part of our visual vocabulary. These are her signatures – sometimes something entirely her own invention; sometimes an existing feature that is redefined forever by being given a Hempel twist. That she is copied so frequently, but so rarely with complete success, is probably down to others' failure to appreciate the thought processes behind her designs, so that most emulators achieve only a superficial likeness. The examples of her work in the following pages will, without doubt, inspire more to attempt to reproduce her magic.

PURELY ORIGINAL

Finally, of course, the secret is that she is not a follower: she is an innovator, an artist who sees the world in a different way. This is a woman of astonishing energy, a life force. Many testify to her fiery temper, her intolerance of what is slipshod; those who know her well speak of her unparalleled loyalty and generosity as a friend, and her zany, surreal, self-deprecating humour. To be in her company is to feel more alive. If she were a car (and it would be a sleek, highly-charged panther of a performance car, capable of startling acceleration), people would want to open up the bonnet to try to find out how she works . . . and they would discover that Anouska Hempel is indeed a one-off: she is wired differently.

COLE PARK IS A COUNTRY HOUSE LIKE NO OTHER. FOR THIRTY YEARS the home of Anouska Hempel and her husband, Sir Mark Weinberg, it is a ravishing yet intricate composition of extraordinary harmony. You will want to dwell on every detail, each room as meticulously thought out as a Covent Garden set by theatre designer Julia Trevelyan Oman. The most magical time to arrive is after dark in winter. The drive begins as a simple farm track across a field. Towards the far side, lines of smooth tree trunks loom into view in the headlights. Suddenly, you are driving along a perfectly formed avenue of ever more impressive length. Teasingly, there is no sign of a house at the end. Amidst the enveloping darkness, lights glimmer faintly some way to the right. A small *rond-point* looms ahead and it is evident that, like a chateau in Normandy, a second perfect avenue leads at right angles to the house.

You are at the gates of a classical house islanded in a square moat, complete with a formal courtyard in front. Swooped baroque gates of silvered oak glide open and the house greets you. Trees around the courtyard are softly lit. Candles glow in every window. As you step through the front door there is an immediate sense of welcome, the light of candles reflected in mirrors and glazed screens.

At dusk a light in every window makes the house warm and welcoming

Many country house entrance halls have a spartan quality with little more than plain wooden chairs ranged around the walls. Here, you step immediately into an inner sanctum, where comfortable sofas and chairs stand close to a blazing fire. The house is the more inviting as every door is open, providing vistas through to a red-curtained study ablaze with light and a dimly lit dining room in shades of green.

The dominant note is a strong architectural discipline, an eye for satisfying shape, symmetry and carefully framed vistas. With this comes a decorator's preference for infinite subtleties in shades of colour and texture, and a collector's love of exotic objects arranged in amusing and theatrical ways. Anouska Hempel talks of layering. At Cole Park the layers have a complexity that in many ways exceeds anything that has gone before. She is the conductor of a symphony in which the craftsmanship and decorative effects play an equal role with the furniture and objets d'art. Many decorators who love flamboyant objects go for a romantic, even Byronic, disarray. Here there is an almost military desire for clean lines and crisp angles all overlaid with such a love of enrichment that the eye constantly dances around the room trying to absorb it all.

The layering is the result of Hempel's enthusiasm for collecting on her travels, combined with the furniture made for the rooms by her long-standing joiner-cum-cabinetmaker, Paul Carter. The brilliance of it all is that very little is fixed. She describes it as 'a hall without walls'. The whole elaborate box of tricks could be quickly packed up and taken away. It is like a three-dimensional chessboard, an assembly of satisfying shapes – cubes, cylinders, spheres – placed symmetrically or in carefully ordered series.

The irregular shape of the hall troubled Hempel from the start. The staircase was not aligned with the front door. The chimneypiece was not centred. The wall opposite was awkwardly stepped forward three times presumably because

Above left: Beyond the formal gravel of the entrance courtyard is a glimpse of lawns
Above: The maturing trees of a closely planted avenue are kept apart to allow a blade of light to streak into the far distance

The view from the bridge across the moat to the front entrance. The grass circle is given interest with distinctive mushrooms of box

The open doors of the entrance hall are precisely aligned with the perfectly formed grand avenue striding into the distance. The bold horizontal stripes of the blinds and carpet are carefully balanced against the vertical shapes of the door, windows and mirrors. Barely an inch of wall is left exposed. Note the framed bird's-eye-view engravings of houses and gardens beneath the windows, echoing the formality and avenues of the Cole Park gardens

ancient masonry could not be moved. Instead of embarking on building works to smooth out these deficiencies, she simply decided to conceal them, using cleverly placed furniture and screens to create a better sense of balance. She explains, 'I want the illusion of walls and things hanging on walls. This house has been got at by so many people. When my work is gone I want someone else to have a chance. So I go for very strong architectural solutions with movable parts.'

Her furnishings in effect create a room within a room. Glazed screens define the central area with the sofas. At the back, further screens, this time her favourite durries, made by prisoners in India, define the boundary between the hall and staircase beyond. An extra dimension is added by the elegantly lettered 18th-century indentures within the glass of the screens, an inspired use of fine calligraphy that usually moulders away in forgotten files. These screens are never set zigzag fashion but always parallel with the walls of the room. 'I love hinges and fiddly bits,' she says.

Beside the doors to the study and dining room is another of her trademarks: slivers of mirror as tall and thin as barometers, beautifully shaped at top and

ANOUSKA HEMPEL

bottom with bevelled glass following the curve, a detail requiring supreme mastery of technique. The hall is given added warmth – like every room in the house – by the brilliant use of lighting. Lights sparkle but never glare. A single large candle glows in the central hanging lamp. Hurricane lamps inset with short square candles multiply the reflections. Table lamps are dark green and opaque, the shape of Chinese conical hats but with white insides that create pools of light on tables and chairs. Nowhere do you see anything so crude as a bare light bulb – translucent discs beneath the shades shield them from view. Further accents are provided by beads of glowing light inside the lattice-fronted library bookcase. This adds a satisfying glint to the gold leaf on bookbindings.

The hall has a subtle heraldic livery with coats of arms over the doors, bordered by pink and beige stripes that are echoed by a matching single pink stripe at intervals on the ceiling. The coat of arms of the Lovell family, ancestral owners of Cole Park, is taken from the fireplace. The stripes are borrowed from the dress of a young girl in a portrait by John Singer Sargent, which hangs to one side of the room.

The entrance hall contains a room within a room, created by the clever placing of screens, which add an instant cosiness. Further warmth is provided by the tall mahogany bookcase rising to the ceiling

Overleaf: Long blinds hang down like veils from the upper landing, picking up the colour of the wall on the left. The fronts of the steps of the staircase are painted to match

ANOUSKA HEMPEL

Above: The swooping handrail subtly contrasts with the strict geometry of rows of favourite Elizabethan portraits, all in matching ebony-black frames. The sitters' dark clothes and backgrounds are set off by the warm red of the walls

Right: Elizabethan ladies in elaborate lace ruffs match the rich decorative treatment of the interior

Opposite: The oak staircase rises round a generous open well to a large balustraded landing. The unpainted wood contrasts with the red of the walls and rugs below

The mirrored screen on the left, with its tall narrow folds, provides multiple reflections of the dining room

An embroidered tablecloth sets off a cluster of oriental baskets

The dominance of the staircase in the entrance hall is muted by placing a three-fold screen in the well of the stair, shielding the banisters from view. Behind the screen hangs a masterfully lit portrait of a boy, which is glimpsed straight ahead of you as soon as you enter the hall. The staircase, dating from 1700 is splendidly robust with a broad swooping handrail and chunky corkscrew balusters. Hempel found it darkened by years of polish. It was not the effect she wanted. Now the wood is pale in tone, showing off the fine carving to even greater advantage. New reversible flourishes have been added, with the fronts of each tread, known as risers, painted a warm pink and the half-landings painted prettily with ribbons.

The staircase is hung with Hempel's Elizabethans – a splendid collection of costumed 16th- and early 17th-century portraits hung close together all the way to the ceiling. They are not individually lit but form a phalanx akin to the close-set portraits in the long galleries of French châteaux, such as Beauregard. Light comes from a pair of tall lamps on a side table on the half-landing. Another nice conceit is the trompe l'oeil picture chains painted on the walls with spiral ribbons, like those on the gondola poles used around the house.

When the Weinbergs first came to Cole Park, the two-tier chimneypiece in the drawing room was set in the end wall. Boldly, Hempel moved the fireplace

to the centre of the long wall, introducing three new tall sash windows at the end so the room now looks over the garden in three directions not one.

Today the drawing room is a symphony in shades of red. These are not the clashing reds that interior designer David Hicks memorably used in his Oxfordshire dining room, but carefully graded warm reds that shade from the orange end of the spectrum, all harmonizing brilliantly. Hempel explains, 'I like using reds. The English would make it yellow with the sun pouring in but that's not the effect I want.' Part of her rationale is to hide the grey weather outside: 'I'm inclined to lower the proportions of the windows, with blinds shutting out the sky at the top.'

Hempel has a phobia of the grand swagged curtains so long fashionable in great houses: 'I can hardly swag a skirt. To me proper swagging is affected and when it's slightly wobbly it doesn't look any good either.' Instead she has taken a cue from a Fortuny belt, placing a circular fan of pleating in the centre of each valance. The curtains are not elaborately double- and triple-lined affairs but simple rolls of complementary fabric suspended from inside the valance, creating her favourite layered effect. These fabrics are from Robert J. Scott, an American with whom she regularly works: 'He has wonderful looms. You simply give them your palette and they make it up.'

This vista to a distant window with daylight bouncing off a tiled floor recalls 17th-century Dutch paintings of interiors

The strong geometry of mullions and leaded panes is set off by a tableau of green succulents and blue and white ceramics

The red drawing room is designed to sparkle in
every light, whether dark and voluptuous in the
evening or brightened by sunlight from south-
facing windows in the day. The scrolled arms
of the Regency settees are emphasized by the
bold stripes of the fabric

Soft lighting in the dining
room picks out highlights
of the green and gold
colour scheme, matched
by prints of exotic plants.
Mirrors reflect details of the
paintings – a grisaille of a
young greyhound seeking
her mother's attention and
two Elizabethan portraits

Above and right: In the kitchen, the patina of a tall oriental cabinet between two windows is picked up by the window seats and blinds, which are here shown half pulled down in classic Anouska Hempel fashion. The polished stone floor reflects the light coming through the mullioned windows

The bold shape of the windows' stone mullions is left unconcealed by curtains and pelmets. Their strong geometry is mirrored in the treatment of the floor and window seats

Above: A love of complexity and layering is evident in this glimpse of a bird bath surmounted by glass storage jars chosen for the patterns of the dried beans and figs inside each one

Left: Porcelain displays are a constant feature of Anouska Hempel interiors. Above the fireplace in the breakfast room, plates are arranged in the form of a Greek cross, while the breakfast table features blue and white pots matching the china in the glazed cupboards behind

The floor of the red drawing room is covered in red and gold herringbone matting: 'These are Indian, made using natural dyes which fade even in candlelight, the reds turning to ginger. If I was as obsessive as I used to be I'd paint the colour back on myself,' she says. The room is as crowded with exotic objects as an oriental emporium. Every tabletop hosts a carefully composed still life. Clusters of objects and piles of books spill onto the floors and under tables and chairs. Among the curiosities is a Japanese red-lacquered pillow, measuring barely a foot across, with a child's still smaller pillow placed on top. 'Japanese pillows are hard. They sleep absolutely straight,' says Hempel. Chinese pots of every shape are marshalled into groups. Chests and trunks sit one on top of another. Grand orangey-red coffee tins, bought in Antwerp, bear the elaborate lettering of Michel et Cie. On tabletops, there are sets of coasters, pot-pourri pots, spheres of flowers. Every conceivable space is used for display.

Looking round the room, the chairs are positioned for conversation. The soft S-scrolls at the ends of the settees contrast with the sabre-legged chairs next to the windows. The doorways into the garden have mirrors set into their sides and tops, creating ladders of reflecting mirrors. Around the dado, and continuing on the panels below the windows, is a set of framed prints of Turkish costumes.

The dining-room lighting is designed to
create a shimmering opulence, playing up
the brilliance of the table setting and its
exquisite crystal and candlesticks with pretty
shades. Note the striped matting emerging
at the end of the table

Hurricane lamps in the dining room are
reflected in the mirrors on the shutters, while
the rows of pots on the floor and sideboard
provide a perfect colour match for the
shimmering silk curtains

The closest attention to detailing is evident in the colour match between the walls, lampshades and table ornaments

The dining room is softer in mood with dark green striped silk curtains and navy blue edging. The fabric hangs in bands catching reflections of the light from the windows. The rich velvet tablecloth has its own livery – a broad-banded stripe running down the centre like a military sash. Beneath the windows are prints of exotic Italian cabbages. 'The stone floor was too blond so we have stained the stone to darken it. We rub die on the stone and then rub it off again. The stone takes colour beautifully,' she says.

For Hempel, eating is an event that must be special at any time of day. The breakfast room, though little more than a corridor, is transformed into a porcelain cabinet, with armorial plates lining the walls and a cluster of Chinese blue and white pots atop the breakfast table. The view through to the kitchen is like an interior by painter Pieter de Hooch, light reflecting on the tiled and stone floors from a window at the end of the room. The kitchen takes its cue from a darkened Japanese tansu chest dating from 1630. 'I found it in an antique shop in Kyoto. I have put legs on to lift it up from the floor,' she explains. It is divided into numerous compartments with drawers and cupboards with reeded sliding doors. An added flourish is provided by tea chests on top. On either side of the kitchen table stand old Japanese garden benches, Shaker-like in their simplicity.

The first-floor landing is furnished in the manner of an Ottoman seraglio. Over the balustrade along the landing are lightweight straw durries lightly sprayed with gold leaf. These are moved up and down according to the season and the weather. There is a constant discussion as to whether the tassels should be removed. The smart pink and grey of the velvet used for curtains and covers is taken from one of the Elizabethans hanging on the wall, a portrait that once hung at Ditchley in Oxfordshire. It is also used on the large divans and the pair of beds standing in the centre of the room. Crispness of line is as important here as in the downstairs rooms. 'I go round kicking things up,' Hempel says, giving a vigorous demonstration of plumping cushions with an elegant shoe.

The guest bedroom by the top of the stairs has a grand baroque state bed made specially for the room. The decor is a bold essay in matt black and gold with matching fabrics in the French fashion, the same striped fabric being used for walls, curtains, valances, bed curtains, bedcovers, chairs and cushions. To give variety the bed cushions are woven with a single wide stripe as if designed to show off some glorious piece of boxed jewelry. Crisp straw matting covers the floor. Shutters are painted black on both sides with mirrors set in the outside panels to reflect light back into the room. The table lamps are black columns with an ivory base and a neck topped by an urn that holds a plain white candle shaft. On the chest tops are trademark spheres of dried red roses and wine coasters.

The bed frame, with it pleated, domed tester, is dramatically tall, almost brushing the ceiling. Furniture includes three chests of drawers, one bought by Hempel, the other two made by Paul Carter to match. Finished in black lacquer, they are inset with 17,500 brass stars. 'I know how many. I had to punch them out with a specially made tool,' says Carter. 'It took four months to do.' Setting the lock in the centre of the gently bow-fronted drawers was an equal challenge. 'I couldn't get the escutcheon dead centre on a standard lock so I had

A tableau at the end of the drawing room
with books, cushions, flowers and fabrics all
chosen for their ravishing pinks and reds

The layered effect is heightened by reflections of a portrait and indentures

Below: Leather bookbindings, lacquer work, a gilt lion's paw and an eagle's wing show how decorative objects can be juxtaposed for effect. Below right: A glazed screen frames a display of ornamental pots seen in a mirror that also reflects another mirror, creating a diagonal vista that is, in part, an illusion

to make them all myself.' He also made the pair of Louis Quatorze-style scroll-arm chairs, copies of one bought by Hempel. The pair of globe mirrors with tendril-like circling arms carrying candleholders are Paul Carter's work, too: 'I build them up with wire and car body filler,' he says.

The bathroom opens at an angle from the corner of the guest room but any awkwardness is immediately dispelled by the brilliant use of woodwork: first the floor-to-ceiling cupboards of the small dressing room grained in imitation of polished mahogany and then the yacht-style boxed-in fittings of the bathroom. An added brilliance comes from the candles that constantly burn on the marble basin tops. The Chinese bedroom next door features another favourite effect: a craquelure on the walls that has the colour and texture of tortoiseshell. Baked, glazed and polished, this technique was learnt from Jim Smart. In the main bedroom the bed stands in the middle of the room. Bed and window curtains have taffeta gathers at the top and burgundy ribbons. Decorative objects include a charming series of Regency-era sailors' Valentines made in Barbados. There are beautifully arranged shells set in charming octagonal boxes. Tall doors are stained on one side to look like mahogany. In the bathroom, toothbrush beakers are made of Scottish horn rimmed in silver.

The attics are a realm of their own, harbouring four guest rooms as well as a central sitting area. When the roof was taken off during repairs, the timbers had to be strengthened or replaced but wherever possible old timbers were kept

and now are all nobly exposed. They stand out like pieces of sculpture, white as driftwood, worn and bent by time. 'I try to be as subtle as possible with my newness,' Anouska Hempel says. All through the attics there are blond scrubbed floorboards in the Scandinavian manner. 'I stencil the edges, using a rope pattern and use straw-coloured fabrics,' she continues. At one end is the Oriel Bedroom overlooking the moat. The bedposts are weathered stone pillars brought from India. The bed curtains are beige linen sheets. 'It's the dusty feel of old French houses,' she explains. In contrast to the lacquered pots in the grand rooms below this is a world of apple-pickers' baskets. The names of the Weinbergs' children are painted over the doors of their bedrooms but there is also a large amount of open-plan space giving a pleasant studio feel, with diagonal roof trusses lending character, as do Hempel's trademark gondola poles.

Faded stencil decoration forms an intriguing pattern on the floorboards in the attics

In the Oriel Bedroom, she continues, 'the colours are chosen to match the moat outside' and a mirror is placed at the back of the bed to make the link. 'This is my pièce de résistance,' says Paul Carter, pointing to the bedhead and matching pelmets. 'They are made from sheets of ply, bent, shaped and carved into bold curved shapes.' Next to the bedroom is a very amusing bathroom painted in the manner of blue and white baroque Portuguese tiles inspired by a panel of real tiles hung over the bath.

'A house must be bedded in the landscape,' says Hempel. To achieve this she uses formal planting with perfect avenues and lines of trees striding out across the landscape in a very Continental manner. 'I cannot do herbaceous borders. It's all little old ladies with their bottoms up in the air.' Over one thousand white horse chestnuts have been planted. 'You won't find a pink one among them,' she says. They come from the Bismarck nursery in Hamburg, owned by the Von Ehren family. 'My gardening is European not English. The Von Ehrens do my planting everywhere. They will grow things for fifteen years and will tell you what is coming up. They taught me how to buy newly moved trees, avoiding the need for ugly posts and wires. You hammer two iron rods diagonally through the root ball. They feed the root as they rust.'

Hempel's long-standing head gardener, Xavier, talks of 'the architecture of trained plants. All the box hedges are spirit-levelled to ensure perfect tops and sides. The wisteria growing up walls is all trained to exact levels so it forms an architectural feature even in winter. If a leaf is out of place it is removed. The lawns must have a perfectly even edge.' The numerous box pompoms are hand cut with clippers or even scissors. 'You don't trim the leaves. You pick out the individual shoots and follow them down, finding the right place to cut. It has to be an overcast day. You are clipping off their protective coat. If there is strong sun, or the day is very cold, it all goes white. We feed the box with blood and bone meal.'

No less important are the perfectly even lines of hawthorn defining the formal garden to the side of the house, each a perfect cylinder in winter as well as summer. 'It's cut using a frame to ensure the tops and sides are even,' says Xavier. He continues, 'We walk the avenues cutting back the branches to the deer line, just above shoulder height.' Interestingly, this is higher than the

The bold handrail and corkscrew banisters of
the staircase are set off by sponged pink walls
and a striped fabric screen that provides an
alcove for a full-length portrait

grazing line left by cattle. Special care is taken over the avenue leading up to the house to ensure the branches do not touch, leaving clear sky between one side and the other. This is done with scaffolding. One of the team stands in a window at the top of the house directing the clipping. In summer a contractor mows the grass in broad stripes.

In the centre of the entrance courtyard is a circle of grass lent distinction by a ring of large box pompoms. For Hempel the big challenge was how to cope with the wing on the left of the house, which, though pleasant enough in itself, spoilt the perfect symmetry of the Palladian façade. The solution was simple and bold – the wing is screened by a line of chestnuts that frame the centre and deflect the eye from the asymmetry. By the corners of the moat are two weathered red-brick pavilions laid in English bond with stone trim and graded roof slates. A graceful serpentine wall connects one pavilion to the house.

The gravel in the courtyard is immaculately raked with a harrow. Overly large stones are picked out by hand as are weeds. Any bits of gravel caught between the paving slabs have to be prized out with a trowel. With the gravel paths in the lawns the challenge is still greater. As the dogs bound round the garden they flick pieces of gravel onto the grass. Before the grass is mown each piece has to be picked up by hand to avoid damage to the blades.

To the south-east of the house the moat is crossed by a delightful Japanese-style bridge, rising in a gentle arc across the water. It is constructed without railings, emphasizing the elegant line, but the deck is formed of old railway sleepers. These have a roughened surface providing good grip in damp weather. Other accents are a splendid Wellingtonia, satisfyingly conical in form, and an ancient yew with spreading bows, which has the spherical shape of a great oak.

The bridge leads to a garden wall cleverly screening the tennis court, complete with stone seats with trompe l'oeil stone cushions. Another new venture is the cathedral, a rectangular enclosure surrounded by beech hedges. In the centre is a 12-metre-long table with a top of dark grey slate. After it has rained a perfectly level film of water sits the entire length of the table as neatly as on the marble edges of the fountains around the Louvre pyramid in Paris.

In the walled kitchen, garden beds are planted with immaculate squares of cabbages. When they sprout, losing their perfect globe shapes, another troupe is already growing to replace them. 'We plant them out on a Wednesday or Thursday ready for the weekend. When it's done it's as if they had never moved,' says Xavier. He continues, 'I ring Blakes and tell them we are sending sage, rosemary, thyme and basil, and Lady Weinberg adapts the menu to include them.' Beside the garden is a handsome ogee conservatory – the well-known model originally designed by the architect Francis Machin. Here Hempel has added extra flourish doubling up the curving ribs.

Cole Park is a house and garden ever in the making. When guests arrive, they always find the furniture rearranged. As the garden grows, so Anouska Hempel's thoughts turn to the wider landscape of hedges, fields and new vistas.

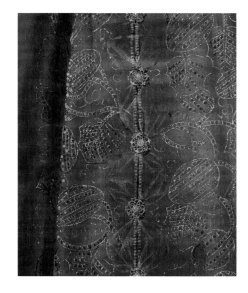

The fabrics of Elizabethan portraits provide the inspiration for the rich textiles used at Cole Park

Above: Red flowers on the Chinese pots match the fabric of the sofas, adding to the intensity and richness of the room

Left: Detail of a portrait on the first-floor landing (see opposite top) with light creating a highly realistic sheen to the painted fabric

Opposite: The first-floor landing, so easily a dead space, here has the richness of an Ottoman seraglio with low red velvet divans. Full-length Elizabethan portraits displaying magnificent costumes match the rich livery of reds. At Cole Park, red comes in many shades and each object is chosen to suit its background

ANOUSKA HEMPEL

Top right: The velvet divan seating runs the length of the landing

Above and right: The cramped space beneath the back stairs is turned into a miniature showstopper by a large chest of pharmacy drawers topped by an ornamental row of wicker baskets. Note the paired lamps and stools

Opposite: In the master bathroom, bath and basin have matching tops that blend with the walls, while mirrors reflecting framed prints increase the sense of space

In the master bedroom, the play of light on luscious folds of fabric and colourful cushions recalls the treatment of drapery in Old Master paintings

Left: The dressing table in the master bedroom consists of a desk with writing flaps extended at each end to display pretty arrangements of small flowers that match the large bowls of snapdragons beneath the windows. Sheaves of golden corn, tied with thick rope, glow beneath the lamps. Below: Objects beneath the tables are chosen and placed with as much care as those on top, adding to the intensity of colour

ANOUSKA HEMPEL

Above: Engraved and gilt decanters with pointed tops, appealing both as a collection and a group, are set on a marble-topped chest of drawers with a miniature ornamental balustrade

Right: A stepped pyramid of suitcases. The stylishness and luxury of travel is a constant theme of Hempel interiors

Below: Highly polished brushes and bootmakers' lasts make up a distinctly masculine tableau

In the guest bedroom, the richness of the bed is increased by repeating the striped fabric on the bedback (with matching bedposts), forming a room within a room hung with its own pictures

Opposite: The choicest *tout ensemble* is created by using the same stripes on the walls as on the bed, with chair cushions matching the bed cover and a gilt mirror reflecting the window curtain

ANOUSKA HEMPEL

Long striped bed curtains settle on the floor like the train of a wedding dress, adding to the opulence of the room

Above: A globe of dried flowers matches the black and gold decor

Left: Window shutters are gilt on the inside to complement the decor, while an ornamental rug provides a perfect colour match

ANOUSKA HEMPEL

The Oriel Bedroom's columned bed resembles a *tempietto*. The columns are diagonally striped similar to Venetian gondola poles. With an impish wit, the capitals of the columns are placed above the frieze, like urns

The broad horizontal blue and white stripes
of the bed covers and blinds at the bay window
are repeated inside the bed canopy and
echoed in the pouf in the foreground of the
Oriel Bedroom

Overleaf: A luxurious bedroom beneath the roof
rafters. Once again, careful colour-matching
creates a *tout ensemble*, with paint, fabrics and
woodwork all in perfect harmony

Pages 66–67: In another attic bedroom, the
triangular geometry of the roof beams forms
a bed setting with a difference, highlighted by
the wedding glow of white pillowcases and
white lamps. Ornamental iron gates create the
impression of an inner sanctum

Above: In this attic bedroom, the reflection of the stone mullion window forms a cross that resembles a crucifix on an altar. The tall candlestick lamps reinforce the impression. Instead of a solid tester, the bed has a shapely baldacchino traced in black wrought iron

Right: Tassels with bow details adorn the windows and blinds

Views of the distinctive Portuguese baroque azulejos in the blue and white tiled bathroom. In the typical Portuguese manner, the tiles are painted to portray complete architectural and pictorial elements, with a pastoral scene in a tapestry-like border on the wall and a dado with cartouche and scrolls beneath the washbasin and bath

Opposite: In the evening, lamps add a golden glow to the guest bedroom's virginal white. Note the birdcage-like light hanging from the top of the ironwork tester

The A-frame roof truss of the attic sitting area has been opened up, revealing how the space was widened at a later
date. A pair of cupboard doors, lime-rubbed to heighten their patina, cleverly divides the space into two seating areas.
The broad floorboards are not varnished but scrubbed in the traditional manner

ANOUSKA HEMPEL

Above: A bay window becomes a work of art beneath a cascade of wisteria, its base enclosed by clipped balls of box. Below: The grass circle in the entrance courtyard is ringed by impressive cushions of box. Opposite: A glazed door opens onto the central garden axis with a gravel path leading to the moat and continuing on the far side with a closely planted avenue

Topiary in an array of
pots clusters around an
umbrella, like guests at
a party, peopling the
garden with varied lively
shapes. The red brick of
the house is transformed
into a green wall by
magnolia and honeysuckle

ANOUSKA HEMPEL

A number of garden tables allows every meal or drink to be taken in a new place, each with its own green table setting and trimmed green backdrop, one with hanging lamps suspended from an ironwork pergola

An aerial view of the house, its moat and gardens. The entrance courtyard is on the left enclosed by trees, with lawns and parterres running down to the moat on the other sides

Neat gravel paths define the shapes of the lawns emphasized by an additional grass border along the edge

ANOUSKA HEMPEL

A quatrefoil garden pool shaded by trees

A dining table between an avenue of lime trees,
pruned into mushroom shapes

The satisfaction of perfect geometric forms:
crisply cut box hedges in matching squares
surround the smaller box squares that frame
the trees. The trees hang low but are clipped
underneath to keep the vista open

ANOUSKA HEMPEL

Above: A trio of obelisks each with an ornamental top

Left: The pale red brick of an English garden wall, built to keep out rabbits and give warmth to ripening garden fruit, now encloses a collection of shapely topiary

ANOUSKA HEMPEL

Right: A garden dining table in a moment of glory, with the wisteria in full flower

Below: The formality of garden walls and hedges is dissolved by a cascade of white wisteria

Tall topiary walls cut into repeating piers form an enclosure known as the cathedral, shown below covered with a marquee, transforming the setting for a spectacular evening banquet

Above: A grand axial vista across a circular pond is framed by stone gate piers

Right: A brick garden wall swoops down to provide a pedestal for a handsome pair of garden urns, matched by another pair in the distance

Smooth stone balls emphasize the edges of pools

The herringbone brick path disappears impressively into the distance while the arch ensures the form of the garden beyond remains a surprise. Turban-topped terracotta finials, as ornamental as Elizabethan chimneys, rise from close-fitting ruffs of box

ANOUSKA HEMPEL

A half-moon garden seat in brick and stone encloses bold architectural paving to form a fan motif in stone, edged with brick. This opens off a herringbone brick path. With the mushrooms of box set in large clay pots, it echoes the felicitous formal garden designs of Sir Edwin Lutyens

A low-set circular pool is satisfyingly enclosed by a large circular wall of dry stone

Left: As the snow melts on the long garden dining table, its top is transformed into a mirror pool. The surrounding black gravel, which has not held the snow, forms a carpet beneath. Trees are lined up on either side like footmen at a banquet

Above: Cole Park seen across the broadest side of
its enclosing moat. Hempel's mushroom-shaped
topiary is picked out in winter by a dusting of snow

Right: A black swan serves as a reminder of
Hempel's favourite colour

MINIMALISM, WHITE, PURE AND COOL

WHEN IT OPENED IN 1997 THE HEMPEL WAS THE MOST DARING AND dramatic transformation of a row of London terraced houses.

The grand stuccoed terraces north of Hyde Park are formed of some of the largest and most opulent town houses ever built in London. Over the years many have become hotels but The Hempel stands out in a class of its own. It is a model of elegant understatement with nothing more than the letter 'H' on each of the pillars of the portico to announce its existence. This is appropriate, for The Hempel is a shrine to minimalism.

As you enter, there is nothing to suggest you are in a hotel at all. The vestibule is bare of furniture, except for a table with orchids, forming a rite of passage from one world to another, in which all normal expectations must be discarded. As if to emphasize this, the door leading into the hotel is not on an axis but in the opposite corner of the room.

New formal paving transforms the garden square in front of the hotel, matching the minimalism of the interior

ANOUSKA HEMPEL

Above: Looking up through the all-white atrium, a much noted feature of the hotel

Left: In the lobby, cornices, skirtings, mouldings and door frames of all kinds have been discarded to create smooth uninterrupted surfaces. Lighting, entering from concealed sources, creates a luminous glow

The large lobby beyond is very different from the grand Italianate architecture outside. The icing sugar white of the walls may be the same, but every moulding has been eliminated to create an aesthetic of crisp volumes and smooth surfaces. There are no skirtings along the edge of the floor, no cornice, no door frames, no mantels to the large fireplaces at either end. To avoid any possible sense of clutter even the seating is set into the floor with steps leading down as into a sunken garden. The sole punctuation mark is a central table with a giant vase in which single white orchids grow out of tall bamboo poles.

Even the fires flickering in the grates are minimalist, with flames mysteriously emerging from a flat gravel shelf. The large chimney breasts containing the fireplaces are faced in blocks of smooth stone, which precisely match the paving of the floor, all intended to create an effect restful to the eye. There are no pictures on the walls, no ornaments. This monastic aesthetic is continued in the sitting room and bar, which open off at either end, and cleverly embraces the plate glass in the sash windows, which can feel bare in traditionally furnished and decorated rooms.

Downstairs, the large dining room has the lofty proportions of the ground floor. By a neat conceit, the walls appear to touch neither the floor nor the ceiling,

Neither a lamp nor a light switch is visible but the rooms glow with light

The two ends of the long transverse entrance hall form a mirror image of each other, with seating areas like sunken gardens and low fireplaces in the end walls. Note the panel of light descending from the atrium

thanks to a recess in place of the usual skirting, painted black so it is invisible against the floor. Another clever trick is the serving table in the centre, which projects a full 2.4 metres into the room without any support.

These mid-Victorian houses had very high ceilings, not just for the sake of grandeur but to allow fumes from gas or oil lamps to rise. Throughout the upper floors, Anouska Hempel makes a virtue of this. The bedroom corridor on the first floor is almost achingly high in relation to its width, but this is turned to advantage by the immensely tall doors that rise from floor to ceiling, creating a serene sense of stateliness. The grandest suites look out over the gardens from the first floor. The Lion's Cage takes its name from a bed suspended on a bridge-like platform by steel rods. A second suite occupies an impressive run of six windows across two former houses. Again, a temple-like effect is created by very tall openings and is emphasized by the thickening of the wall between the sitting room and the bedroom beyond. Another clever architectural touch is provided by a square ceiling band that accentuates the satisfying shape of the room like a carpet border.

This sense of style is carried through to more standard rooms. Room 105 on the first floor shows an insistent desire to achieve a symmetry worthy of a Renaissance architect. As the door opens you enjoy a carefully framed vista running the length of the apartment. As you reach the central seating area, a cross-axis opens up, again symmetrical on either side. The bed is placed exactly on an axis to the left while opposite a pair of sofas sit on either side of a television, which can disappear into a white box if its presence detracts from the calm.

It is the same in the bathroom beyond. The basin stands centrally at the end, like a font in a church, with its glass bowl set on a plinth of exactly the same dimensions. Again there is a cross-axis, with the bath placed centrally on the right and nothing more than a tall plate radiator opposite, that is until you see the lavatory and bidet placed symmetrically on either side. The wit lies in the neatness of it all with cleverly hidden lighting bouncing off the cove of the bathroom ceiling back into the sitting area.

Fiercely stark minimalism is brought to life by
bright, but not glaring, light that picks out
shades of black and grey

Above: To ensure smoothness of surface, the legs and backs of the chairs in the I-Thai restaurant are concealed in all-white covers, leaving only the slender table legs visible. The walls and ceiling are bare but lit up by star-like lights and circular spots

Right: The theme is carried through into the smaller dining rooms

THE HEMPEL

Above: Plain walls and ceiling contrast with the planes of the floor and low-level furniture – the decorative answer to a detox. Below left: A staircase without risers is light and transparent. As mouldings are anathema in such a space, the handrail is indented. Below right: The strong, simple shape of a kimono fills an otherwise bare wall like a picture

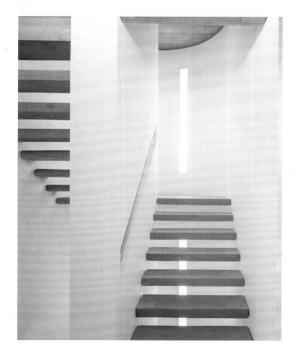

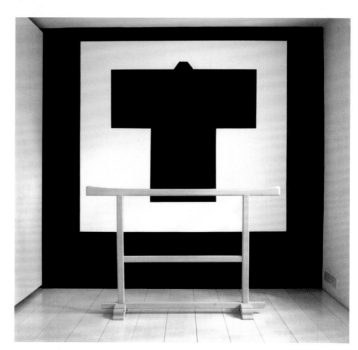

In a minimalist hotel, variety from one room to another is all the more important and challenging. Clever play is made with constant variations in the restricted palette of black, grey and white. Furniture is designed to provide the simplest of shapes

All-white upholstery is matched by the orchids
on the window sills

The fringe of the throws draped on the chairs is the sole decorative detail to have escaped the ruthless culling of all other superfluous detail

Above: An interior as carefully composed and layered as a Cubist painting. The straight lines of the floorboards and doorway are set off by the shallow curve of a porcelain bowl and the soft shapes of a bed

Left: Baths and basins follow bespoke designs that maintain the crisp lines and pure forms of the hotel interior

ANOUSKA HEMPEL

Black and white bedrooms are dressed as if
for Cecil Beaton's Ascot scene in the 1964 film
My Fair Lady

In the Lion's Cage suite, the floating bed
levitates from the floor with Zen-like perfection.
The stainless steel poles form a screen that
provides some privacy from the outside world

A minimalist four-poster bed with pure lines standing in for the traditional hangings. Note the gently tapering posts, fabric-covered bedhead and tall, slender reading lamps

The dark frontage with white steps and window trim sets an immediate note of chic

IF BLAKES WAS A STAGE SET, THE AUDIENCE WOULD ERUPT INTO applause as soon as the curtain went up. From the cord carpets and cane hand-rails to the lovebirds in the hall, Anouska Hempel has created a novel, exotic world, contrived to make you alternately gasp and smile in delight.

The word often used about Blakes is decadence, reflected in an abundance of black and gold. But naturally there is choice: the cool white muslins of the Corfu Suite, popular for honeymoons; the explosion of reds in the Cardinal Suite; the white and beige Pasha Room where the canopy over the bed is supported on tent poles and the divans sunk into the floor. Or the 007 Suite 'licensed' for weddings and furnished with Syrian mother-of-pearl furniture.

Hempel bought what she calls a rooming hotel in London's South Kensington in 1974. It opened quietly four years later, propelled to fame by her fireball energy and dazzling charisma. It has been acclaimed many times as the first boutique hotel. Hempel explains, 'The magic was that every room was different. It had everything I loved from around the world. We began with two houses and an old leather sofa. I was barman and housekeeper. We started to attract people who wanted a Bohemian milieu. The rich would pay a fortune but others I'd let stay for free at the last moment.'

She continues, 'I was doing commercials and these were the days when advertisements brought repeat fees. The money paid for the roof and allowed me to go to a bank and borrow against my fantastic earnings. I used to get repeat fees. It was £25,000 for smoking a cigarette. As money came in, I put it into the business. It felt like a country house in England or Italy or a swanky suite in Manhattan. Blakes had a romance, as if I had spared no expense. It felt lush and rich, as if it belonged somewhere else in time, as in a dream.'

Hempel recalls, 'We had four separate entrances to protect everyone's privacy. Some guests signed in. Some did not. It was an era when everyone was taking chances and up to mischief. It became a hangout for all kinds of creative people.' Progressively, she bought three more houses.

A bronze bust in front of a red woven basket in the dining room

One piece of early advice was that guests would have jet lag. She was told, 'You can't allow a chink of light to disturb them.' Hempel responded with tall, thick curtains with multiple folds. 'I would make a bed and sell ten of them. It was huge fun. We were all young and had no training. I bought engravings, never copies.' Some of her collections of exotic objects are now so rare that museums have expressed interest in them.

A Director's Double comes with mustard ceiling and black walls, hung with prints of London squares in glistening gold frames. You cannot imagine there are so many Georgian squares in London, until you realize that some of the prints are repeated two or three times to create the architectural effect (as are the engravings of gods and goddesses in the bathroom) always, to be noted, perfectly in line. This doubling and tripling, combined with constant layering, is

A London terrace is dramatically transformed by the unifying paint scheme that identifies the capital's first and foremost boutique hotel. Apart from the neatly clipped pots on the first-floor balcony, there is barely a hint of the sensational interiors within

a signature of Blakes. Occasional tables come in pairs with twin lamps on them, pictures are triple-banked, towels sit or hang in threes, the bath mats are laid on top of both a printed rug and a plain rug, all matching the colours of the room. On maple wood chairs sit beautifully plumped satin cushions – one black, one mustard – while at the foot of the bed cushions (diminishing in size) wittily form twin pagodas, which remain even when the bed is made up for the night.

There is an abundance of clever and amusing decorative techniques at Blakes. Ornamental parquet floors are stencilled onto the plain floorboards, bathrooms are miniature print cabinets with engravings of British worthies

The entrance lobby evokes the age of elegant travel, with trunks serving as tables and an umbrella shading a ship's gangway stair whose cane handrails descend to the bar

pasted directly on the walls and even transferred onto the window glass as a kind of modesty screen. In the Cardinal Suite the red brocade valances to both bed and windows are as rich as altar frontals in a Roman baroque church. Walls painted in imitation of tortoiseshell add to the gorgeous effect. Colourful flower prints are hung from pink silk ribbons tied in bows at the top. A cleverly chosen late 17th-century painting of songbirds and baskets of red cherries completes the symphony in scarlet.

The basement lounge is a divanned seraglio but the decorative theme is set by a six-fold Chinese Coromandel lacquer screen. Placed flat on the wall like a

Above: The six-fold lacquer screen
in the Chinese Room, which is in the
basement and often referred to as the
'Opium Den'

Right: Details of exotic birds on the
Chinese lacquer screen

tapestry, this has earned the room the sobriquet of the 'Opium Den'. The screen's ornamental border is continued round the room and carefully matched in broad bands of grey and salmon-pink cotton fabric hung on the walls and used for seats and cushions – with stripes of varying width to avoid monotony. A gently insistent geometry creates a satisfying sense of order with low square lacquer tables divided into quarters by red beading and stacked with books topped by oriental boxes. Here you can sip a 'Cigdem' cocktail, a blend of ginger, melon and sake topped up with champagne, and sample beluga canapés served in glass boxes on black lacquer trays. The same livery continues in the atmospherically dark dining room with chairs and tablecloths all in matching fabric. Napkins, neatly dressed with ginger and black ribbons, complete the ensemble.

The garden, a miniature forest of tubs of clipped box and bay trees, provides another stylish retreat in which to enjoy a drink or a meal. The whole transformation is so theatrical that guests leave the daily grind of London pavements as soon as they cross the threshold. Blakes is a modern version of the proverbial magic carpet, which in an instant whisks you to a distant opulent world.

The sense of richness in the Chinese room is heightened by the bands of salmon pink edged in grey on the tables, chairs and seating. Low banquettes around the walls and an abundance of cushions create the feeling of an oriental divan

Above: The table setting echoes the room's
decor right down to the napkins, which are
tied in ribbons of alternating colours

Opposite top: A circular dining table is
decorated with anemones, chosen because
they perfectly match the tropical flowers that
decorate the top of the lacquer screen in
the background

Opposite bottom and overleaf: In the basement
bar, exotically painted, elongated stick figures
are just one of the many elements transporting
the visitor to a world of excitement far away
from the London streets upstairs

ANOUSKA HEMPEL

Clockwise from top right: An oriental portrait is a perfect colour match for the walls; decorative inlay with a vase of flowers and the winged chimera of Greek mythology; decorative elements from around the world are used throughout the hotel; orchids, fans and oriental armour gently hint that this is a home for seasoned travellers

Opposite: Black is dominant within Blakes, usually combined with shades of one other colour to add brilliant contrast and lustre

The dining room alternates its black and
white table settings, while a sense of depth
is increased by the clever use of shadow
and mirrors

A bedroom suite with purple walls and floor and blond neo-classical furniture. The swan-armed settee is framed by matching pier tables and double-banked architectural prints on the wall behind

The green and gold of the bed hangings and cushions is matched by the leather bookbindings and set off by a painted floor that resembles a chessboard

Opposite: Leather-bound books filling floor-to-ceiling bookshelves turn a lobby into a library

A folding screen with a panoramic scene
of dreamy spires provides the backdrop for
monochrome fabrics set off by pretty flowers
(with matching ribbon) and preserved plants

Opposite: The sheer number of carefully
chosen decorative objects and books suggests
that you are a guest in a very sophisticated
private house

ANOUSKA HEMPEL

Dark walls set off blond furniture and brilliant
saffron-yellow fabric to startling effect. Similar
shades are found throughout Blakes

Right: A trio of traditional Chinese bamboo
stacking food baskets

Opposite: Apricot and sapphire blue curtains
create a blaze of colour in a bedroom

The Cardinal Suite has sumptuous red brocade valances on the four-poster bed and the windows, with matching bedback, sofa, chairs and cushions. The exotic framed flower prints maintain the vivid colour scheme

The reds of the lacquer pots and table, striped barber's-pole posts to the bed and velvet
cushions emblazoned with the fleurs-de-lis of France all harmonize perfectly

ANOUSKA HEMPEL

Overleaf: Rich, satin bed hangings are reflected in a large dressing-table mirror, emphasizing
their match with both the window curtains and the tortoiseshell of the walls

A Napoleonic boat bed, adorned by gilt sea
horses and cornucopia shells, is flanked by
drum-shaped bedside tables with scrolled
Ionic capitals supporting the square tops

Opposite: The bold horizontal stripes of
a bedhead are paired with diagonally striped
cushions and a pleated top

Pairs of tall bamboo lights with Chinese coolie
shades stand on the desk and the side table
in the room beyond. Note the grouping of
objects: three cushions on the chair, a set of
globe-shaped candles and a highly theatrical
gilt trophy over the door

ANOUSKA HEMPEL

A dark blue, oval slipper bath has a border painted on the floor, while the mirror behind reflects
a pair of mirrors on the opposite wall as well as the domed ceiling

Above and below: A tented encampment is the inspiration for the Pasha
Room, its sand-coloured stripes reminiscent of both desert and beach

Above: A bathroom with sponged grey walls that match the grisaille
tones of the prints

In the 007 Suite, the pale beiges, taupes and ochres of the
floor and walls allow the bed furnishings to float. Twin chests
of drawers richly inlaid with mother-of-pearl match the
folding chairs at the foot of the bed. The scrubbed wooden
floor, white bed and window curtains intensify the lightness
of the room

Right: A mirror carved with oriental geese creates infinity
reflections. Below: An ornamental ring of dried flower heads

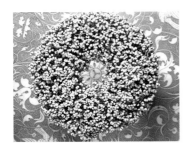

Left: Trompe l'oeil decoration in the baroque style with dolphin supporters to a circular window

Below and opposite: A corridor painted with faded architectural motifs, including giant urns and a scrolled pediment over the door. Scrubbed floorboards echo those in the painted interiors of Scandinavian houses

Left: Patterns in art and nature: a trio of balls similar to dried onions' heads are set on a background of trailing foliage complete with songbird

ANOUSKA HEMPEL

Sofa, cushions and curtains in a matching white fabric look positively ethereal when the sun streams through the windows in the Corfu Suite

ANOUSKA HEMPEL

Above: A pair of mirrors on the end wall subtly increases the apparent length of the room. The pictures are hung in matching groups of six while the chimneypiece is richly carved with swags of fruit and flowers. Below: The broad horizontal stripes of the walls are set off by the two-tone fabric of the curtains and tall glazed bureau topped with pots that touch the cornice. Striped cushions on the armchairs echo the tablecloth and loose cushions around the window

ENLIVENED BY THE PLAY OF LIGHT

THE ELEGANT STUCCOED TERRACES NORTH OF HYDE PARK STOOD AS sleeping beauties for much of the 20th century, many converted to bedsits and cheap hotels during the Great Depression of the 1930s and post-war austerity. Yet their remarkable good looks lived on even in genteel decay. Developers in the 1960s eyed up the area for demolition, but the great battle for London, begun in the 1970s, saved Bayswater and ensured it remained one of the capital's most complete and harmonious neighbourhoods, similar to the brownstones of the Upper East Side in New York. The stuccoed houses of Inverness Terrace were listed as 'buildings of special architectural interest' in 1970 and a conservation area was declared.

Since then nearby Notting Hill has grown to celebrity status. Its revival was followed by those of Tyburnia and Bayswater, the latter named after Bayard's Watering Place, recorded in the year 1380 as a place where horses could drink from a stream later called Bays-water. In the early 19th century, artists and writers were attracted to this new district that was still half rural. By 1862 'a great and aristocratic town' had grown up, faster than all other suburbs, according to the Survey of London. Houses were well built and enjoyed good air in contrast to the recently 'ill-drained' marsh of Belgravia. By 1882 the increasingly cosmopolitan suburb boasted a Greek Orthodox cathedral in Moscow Road and a synagogue in St Petersburgh Place.

Anouska Hempel helped spark the area's fashionable revival with the hotel that bears her name. At The Hempel she took a row of tall white stuccoed terraced houses and transformed them into a temple to Minimalism that became famous around the world. La Suite West, her new hotel in Inverness Terrace, which opened in 2012, is installed in a similar row of houses. This time they overlook not a leafy square but a traditional street, narrow enough to ensure the traffic slows, making it feel secure and even intimate.

Hempel transformed the terrace by bringing trees and shrubs back into the front gardens – where others park their cars – with her trademark formal gardening. Beneath a canopy of plane trees, tables are laid out invitingly for alfresco eating and drinking.

Planes, of course, are a staple of London streets, the only trees that could withstand the stifling London smogs. Here they are as carefully chosen as guardsmen, slender and ramrod straight and standing in perfect rows. Around them are smart black pots with tapering sides from which balls of box, with even more slender trunks, grow to precarious heights.

Each group of planes forms an umbrella clipped into a square canopy. The tables and benches have no legs: the smooth blond tops of American oak simply descend at right angles to form solid supports. Hurricane lanterns half as tall as telephone boxes stand on the tables. These clean, insistent lines are the leitmotif of the hotel and are used to emphasize both height and length.

The hotel's reception area is a novel play on a minimalist theme, using exaggerated line to create a distinctive look

Though the houses retain their handsome columned porches – all identical – none of them alone provided the drama Hempel required. The grand entrance is at the end of the terrace. You must look hard to spot a name plate on the low wall. As at The Hempel, the first impression on entering is of pure, bare space signifying the entrance to another world, a place of sanctuary quite distinct from the street outside. It is deliberately low key so there is little to alert the uninvited.

The sole touch of pomp is the six-metre-tall door standing open at exactly 90 degrees. This is the more apparent as it turns not on hinges but on a pivot secured in the floor and ceiling sufficient to its considerable weight, moving effortlessly at a gentle push. Bare white walls give nothing away – light descends from windows that are out of sight onto black paving slabs that reflect the gleam from above.

Only at the very end do you turn to see a welcoming white marble reception desk. Dramatically, this runs the full seven-metre-length of the space unsupported from below. The monastic walls and black floor continue. Clutter is strictly banished – sliding doors screen from view all the customary sights of hotels, whether racks of keys or pigeonholes for post. Opposite is the one concession to a weary traveller, a long low bench with live flames glowing in the centre from a minimalist grate. The busy life of the street is also kept at bay by the slatted screens in the front windows. The transformation is as complete as in a traditional Japanese inn, or ryokan.

As in Japan, intimacy is created by the lack of open public spaces where guests might congregate. On the way to your room you pass a discreet restaurant

Plain all-white surfaces are enlivened by the play of natural light across them

An architectural rendering of La Suite West shows the rhythm of the individual townhouses. The columned porticoes are cleverly picked up on by squares of pleached plane trees that run the length of the generous front gardens

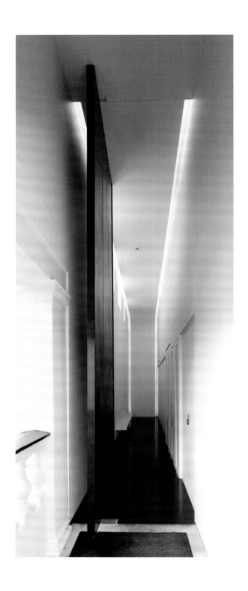

with comfortable sofa tables on either side and another black slatted screen providing seclusion from the world outside – beyond are tables opening onto the garden. The same strict simplicity is maintained in the restaurant but the walls are decorated with rows of matching mirrors in emphatic black frames that highlight the symmetry.

The livery repeats in the bedroom corridors. Great care has been given to creating distinctive groups of rooms for diverse budgets, taking advantage of the varying aspect and outlook of rooms on different floors and the special character of those that open out onto the ground-floor gardens and the roof terraces.

Four-poster beds have long been a trademark of Hempel's hotels. At The Hempel she pioneered the minimalist four-poster, echoing beds in the Caribbean where the presence of drapes would be breathless and hot. Here, the pure lines of the frame transforms the bed into a temple. It is an effect that needs panache to carry it off without looking mean. It is done in the classic French manner of designing every element to match: pairs of black-framed mirrors coordinate with the bedframe and a black facing to the doorway into the bathroom. Carefully placed lighting picks out accents of colour, such as purple cushions on white pillowcases.

Another flourish comes with the bathrooms. While white marble bathrooms with gold taps and brass towel rails have become a cliché, here veined marble is turned to stunning effect by creating patterns in the manner of marbled end papers in a well-bound book. It is achieved by splitting the marble into thin veneers so the pattern repeats four ways in a diamond shape. It is all the more

Left: Drama is added on arrival by an immensely tall door turning on a pivot. Arcs of light invite you to walk to the inner entrance at the back

The reception area features a hearth and bench seat that extend the length of the wall

ANOUSKA HEMPEL

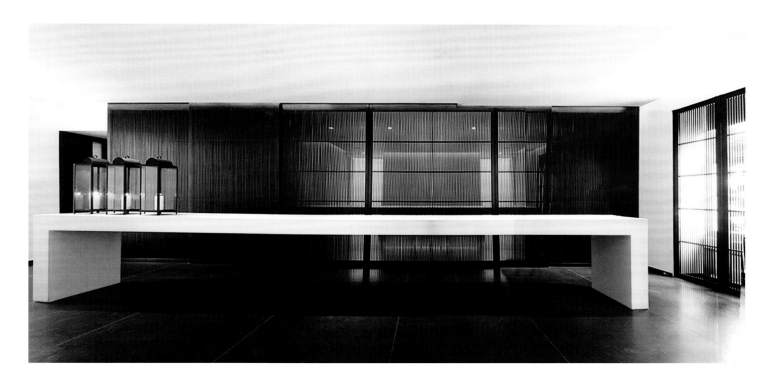

effective – and pure – thanks to the minimalist aesthetic of eschewing handles, mouldings and projections. Mirrors multiply the effect, reversing the pattern.

Anouska Hempel's hotels have always been acclaimed for their food as much as their design. La Suite West is no exception and even afternoon tea, with its classic finger sandwiches, comes with a new twist – cucumber with hummus, rocket and red onion slices, tomatoes and Portobello mushrooms, scrambled tofu and spicy guacamole, and roasted spinach and cauliflower mousse. A sparkle has been added to a well-loved tradition.

The front desk is kept clear of clutter to show off its dramatic length, achieved without any intermediate supports

Concealed lighting and smooth surfaces shorn of all mouldings reinforce the minimalist rigour

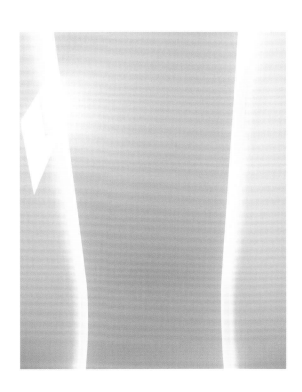

Above and opposite: A pair of free-standing
lattice screens creates the sense of a room
within a room. Note how reflected daylight
turns black surfaces to white

Narrow but inviting gangway stairs recall those
that enter the tail of a large aeroplane

ANOUSKA HEMPEL

A four-poster bed with a lattice-screen bedhead
and matching mirrors all edged in black

Bathrooms are faced in marble chosen for its beautiful veining and split to create symmetrical patterns that are multiplied in the mirrors

A stack of paving stones awaiting laying attests to a passion for fine natural building materials

The hotel's pure lines and surfaces are reflected in a mirror-smooth pool, with palm trees adding a tropical note in the distance

EMERGING FROM THE CANOPY OF A BRAZILIAN RAINFOREST, WARAPURU looks down to a spectacular beach of golden sand and aquamarine sea, which turns to turquoise as the waters of the Atlantic rapidly deepen.

The resort is a project on a heroic scale, intended to offer a degree of hedonism to thrill even the most seasoned beachcomber. It is to be a classic Bond-film lair, the equivalent of the mountain-top eyries and lagoon grottoes favoured by the films' villains. It is described by Anouska Hempel Design as 'minimalist-monolithic' – bold enough in form to respond to the majestic setting but substantially screened by mature trees and vegetation. From both the sea and surrounding hills, the great cloak of rainforest remains pristine and unsullied by development.

The concept for Warapuru is of a resort hotel with cabanas and pavilions set in groups at either end of the beach, concealed among the plentiful palm trees, and private bungalows high up the hillside at a level with a hotel. The dense rainforest reserve all around is a UNESCO World Heritage Site.

Guests will either arrive on the private landing strip next to the hotel or by flying into Ilhéus via Rio de Janeiro or São Paulo. A vast entrance hall formed of blond travertine will greet them on arrival. This is fronted by a black basalt reflection pool that serves as a roof for the spacious reception room below. The two reception desks are flanked by a matching pair of fireplaces set into the end piers, as at The Hempel in London. Visitors will emerge to see the sparkling cove 90 metres below. The forty hotel rooms are in private cabanas or pavilions built of stone or timber, and range from 160 to 330 square metres. Each will have its own pool and sun deck.

The design unfolds as a series of breathtaking spaces and terraces, each providing a new panorama or vista. Surprise and delight await at every turn. The aesthetic mixes the oversailing roofs and terraces of Frank Lloyd Wright's famous Pennsylvania house, Fallingwater, and the almost monastic simplicity of The Hempel. But it goes several stages further, taking advantage of the tropical location to dissolve the barriers between indoor and outdoor space. The spa downstairs, with its sloping walls cloaked in grass, has the character of a camouflaged fort with window openings as muscular as gun embrasures.

Hempel's love of a grand axis takes flight in the sweeping broad, shallow steps to the Beach Club below. The Club is half Mayan temple, stepped up in three stages, and half Mies van der Rohe's Barcelona Pavilion, with smooth walls descending into mirror pools of water. The first level contains a swimming pool partly shaded by the overhang of the terrace above, which hosts a restaurant and bar with elevated views in the shade or sun, as guests prefer. Bold horizontal lines embed the Beach Club in the surrounding landscape.

Warapuru lies south of the city of Itacaré, which was once a small indigenous Indian settlement, surviving on hunting, fishing and farming. Colonization began in 1530 and with the Portuguese came the Jesuits, who erected a chapel in 1720. Early accounts record constant Indian attacks. As a result, the Jesuits decided to build a tunnel connecting their monastery to the church, where they could retreat to safety. For years the wealth of the southern Bahia region lay in cocoa plantations but, when these were in economic trouble in the 1970s, the focus shifted to tourism and serving the surfers who were beginning to discover these then hard to reach beaches.

Now Itacaré is alive with seafront hotels and pousadas. Portuguese hotelier João Vaz Guedes initiated Warapuru's implementation in 2004, but work came to a halt a few years later due to the financial crisis. In this spectacular location, with the main construction work already finished, it must soon attract the new investment needed for its completion.

When wet, the polished black stone reflects the sky and trees beautifully

The strong overhang of the balcony provides deep shade below

Digital rendering of the hotel's dramatic position level with the rainforest canopy, eighty-five metres above the beach

Digital rendering of the Beach Club set fifteen metres above the beach with a thirty-five-metre-long swimming pool surrounded by timber sundeck. On the first floor is a panoramic restaurant and bar

Above: A tall pivot door stands open at a right angle, revealing a view to the terrace beyond

Floor-to-ceiling glass walls and thrusting terraces bring guests to eye-level with the rainforest canopy, with a glimpse of the sea beyond

Sun terraces inset with pools of palest aquamarine water have the satisfying look of all being hewn from the same stone. The unusually broad sides to the balconies provide an additional place to sit

Above: A cabin, providing seclusion and shade, is formed like an ornamental box and given visual strength by the extra panels on the roof and sides

The floors and walls of the cabin are all of the same dark wood providing a contrast with the intense sun outside

Above: Terrace, pool and balustrade are all faced in the same beautifully textured stone, creating an intense purity of form and sense of harmony

The pattern of sunlight on the floor is as crisp as the lattice panels on the walls

Above: A grand but minimalist ascent gives no hint to where it leads thanks to enclosing walls and concealed lighting on the landing

Left: The minimalist aesthetic is evident in smooth surfaces free from cornices, skirtings, mouldings or projections of any kind

Opposite: Walls, floors and staircase are all faced in the same travertine stone. Each is treated differently to create subtle contrasts

Overleaf: A bedroom with sliding plate-glass windows that open out onto a bridge spanning a bathing pool

ANOUSKA HEMPEL

Intense discipline and rigour ensure that shelves and recesses for hanging clothes exactly match
the doorways and screens, with a skylight illuminating the bed from above. Below: Basin set in
a slab of marble with concealed lighting

ANOUSKA HEMPEL

Doors pivot to avoid the intrusion of door frames. Solidity vanishes, making way for an ethereal lightness

The hotel's narrowboat going to fetch guests

In the reception a pair of giant drum
lampshades reinforce the smart black livery

FROM THE DAY IT OPENED IN 1999 BLAKES AMSTERDAM WAS A
destination in itself, a theatrical experience that began the moment you stepped
through the imposing Doric-columned portico. Blakes stands on Amsterdam's
noblest canal, the Keizersgracht, or Emperor's Canal, named for the Holy Roman
Emperor, Maximilian I. It was dug in the early 17th century, Holland's Golden
Age, and is today included on the UNESCO World Heritage List.

In an earlier incarnation, No. 384 was indeed a theatre, though it burnt to the
ground in 1772. The wings had caught fire during a performance of the opera
The Poorly Protected Daughter and within fifteen minutes the entire building had
been ablaze. Blakes Amsterdam was a shooting star of equal brilliance, attracting
a fashionable clientele; it has now been rebranded The Dylan with some change
to its original character.

Anouska Hempel played up the dignity and fabric of the historical building
while imbuing it with a new electricity and atmosphere. She says, 'I'm a
conservationist at heart, so I didn't want to lose any of the house's quality.' The
1617 theatre had been set back, behind a courtyard opening off the street. The
leading Dutch architect Jacob van Campen had built it in emulation of Andrea
Palladio's famous Teatro Olimpico in Vicenza.

The 1772 fire was hailed as the work of Satan by opponents of the theatre
and the site was bought by a leading Catholic charity, the Office for the Aged
and the Poor. No. 384 was transformed to serve the organisation's needs; it even
included a bakery and a storehouse for grain flour and peat. The governors of
the charity were wealthy men and they demanded the same tall windows and
splendid doorways that characterized their own homes.

In 1975 the building was restored mundanely as offices. Over twenty years
later, a new owner, planning a conversion to luxury apartments, began to think
the building deserved more. His eureka moment came at Blakes London, where
behind another plain brick front he found a temple to the decorative arts – and
one with the *koloniaal* feel that so appeals to the Dutch – with bamboo, umbrellas
and Louis Vuitton trunks. He invited Hempel to Amsterdam and in the first two
minutes a vision of the new hotel began to form in her imagination.

She recalls:'In a private house I am concerned with my client. A hotel can be
exactly as I want it to be. I'm designer and management. This is my environment.
It's a great building, tall aristocratic proud.' This was the era when Amsterdam
was casting off its *Burgherlich* image, and a new generation alive to the pace of
New York, Paris and London wanted to stay in more stylish, edgy, smart hotels,
providing a window onto another world. *Frommer's Guide* quipped: 'You'll surely
observe more males with ponytails than on a Kentucky stud farm.'

Hempel wanted to travel back in time as well as forward. The spice trade of
the Dutch East India Company inspired the colours of ginger and turmeric for
bedrooms. She wound lamps and 'jousting' poles with grosgrain ribbon. The

Above: The dramatic entrance portico is given emphasis with clipped topiary. Left: Looking into the inner courtyard

deep shadows and candlelight of Dutch baroque paintings lent an atmosphere that fit perfectly with her love of black. Blue and white china dazzled like the shipwrecked Nanking cargo. The discipline of a William and Mary garden was brought to the courtyard. She made a virtue of the tall ceilings, which ten years before designers would have masked to create intimacy and cosiness. She describes the umbrellas in the garden courtyard as the black sails of a few Flying Dutchmen passing through.

The restaurant opened in the old bakery; the ovens remain in the brick wall. Guests warmed to the signature details of screens and old lacquered trunks, and above all to her trademark tall four-poster beds and linen sheets. One guest exclaimed: 'Ours was green – on entering, I actually shouted: "Wow!" An enormously tall double bed on which were piled twelve cushions arranged in groups of three, several trunks piled on top of each other and a minibar which even contained oxygen.'

The inner courtyard's square umbrellas match the squares in the paving, all graded in colour to match the painted walls

The twenty-six bedrooms, later extended to forty-one, were grouped by colour. Some came in ginger, set against slate grey with a thin line of turmeric to add zest. Others were the navy and black of kimonos. Rooms off the garden courtyard offered the greens of lavender and rosemary while those under the eaves were an airy beige and white, as at Cole Park. Through the labyrinth of corridors, colour helps guests return to their rooms.

Great care was given to controlling light in the bedrooms, using sliding slatted screens, linen panels, adjustable window blinds and curtains. 'I want that kind of control. I provide it for my guests, but if pulling screens around is not for them they can enjoy it just as I have left it,' she continues. Minibars were stocked with canisters of oxygen for a pick-me-up, and Berocca anti-stress vitamins, ginger chocolate, sleep masks, an energy drink and candles scented with grapefruit or amber were supplied. Hempel likes cameras, so there was one in every room.

Staff were taught how to place each glass, coffee pot and sugar bowl precisely on its own square of slate, to maintain the careful geometry of every table

setting. The hotel became popular so quickly that it was not easy to get a room or a table for dinner, and people who knew her hotels in London were suddenly thinking it would be nice to take a trip to Amsterdam. 'If people like what I do, that pleases me,' said Anouska Hempel. 'It's my total world, my whole life, that they're coming to.'

The old is revealed and burnished to show it to best advantage, whether plain brickwork or solid roof beams. Vistas and symmetry create the formality she loves. 'I constructed a bath on a balcony over a bedroom to use the space beneath the rafters. The water gushes out through a horizontal slot and emerges like a waterfall,' says Hempel.

Her characteristic iron discipline is everywhere apparent. She laughs: 'The champagne tastes the same if you're sitting bolt upright or sunk back into a sofa, so you might as well be upright, because you look better.' Or, as one guest put it, 'If Amsterdam wasn't so beautiful, I'd be happy to stay in the red oriental bedroom all day.'

Grouped architectural prints of triumphal arches and tempiettos stand out from the dark walls and furniture. The simplicity is matched by the wide floorboards sanded in the traditional manner to provide a blond finish that glows in direct sunlight

In Holland, as in England, the sash window gives a verticality and distinctive pattern to every wall and enfilade, here matched by the angular shapes of screens seen through the internal window

Left: Pale green hydrangeas add a flash of brilliance to the black livery

ANOUSKA HEMPEL

Above and below: In darkened rooms, pools of light draw attention to the fabric of inviting sofas, the pattern of vintage glazed floor tiles and artfully arranged ceramics

Below: Dozens of small lights pick out the colour of the walls and floor and create reflections in the glass on the tables

In the restaurant, a note of smartness and luxury is struck by the low white upholstered armchairs, which fit the room as snugly as if they were on a yacht. Tall mirrors lengthen the room with matching reflections of lamps

Left: Classic film stills discreetly projected onto the wall add a sophisticated period note

ANOUSKA HEMPEL

The textured surfaces of the brick walls and tiled floors of the
restaurant contrast with the creamy white linen seat covers and
black tables. Tall lampstands are marshalled like a row of attendant
footmen, their numbers multiplied in the mirrors

BLAKES · AMSTERDAM

A space contrived beneath the eaves is made
chic by painting the roof beams jet black to
match the bath surround, while a touch of
colour is added by the blue and white
Dutch china

Lamp nods at lamp to emphasize the perfect
symmetry and elegant line of a minimalist
four-poster bed, which is without drapes but
adorned with artful stacks of cushions

ANOUSKA HEMPEL

An extravaganza of stripes creates dazzling glamour, enriched by the clever contrasting patterns – broad and narrow, vertical and horizontal

Opposite: A four-poster in the oriental manner with a screen back. Slender vertical supports provide an elegant contrast to the bolder ceiling beams, which are painted to match the floor matting

THE CREATION OF A LOOK HAS ALWAYS BEEN A SINGULAR STRENGTH OF Anouska Hempel's work. Blakes, her first hotel creation, grew to splendour in stages. The Grosvenor House Apartments sprung upon the world – all 130 of them, perfectly honed in every detail. Jumeira Hotels, who also own the Burj Al Arab in Dubai, pride themselves on elegance and luxury, and here offer exceptional comfort and visual harmony, subtly varied from one suite to another. Each room has a bespoke feel, tailor made and not just a standard product.

Like classic ocean liners, Grosvenor House has a livery distinct from every other hotel in London. It is all black or all grey, or rather a clever palette of shades of black – or grey – in each apartment. Yet each comes with an accent of brilliant colour – orange, tangerine or marmalade – standing out in luminous contrast. Black, in the hands of a true artist, is a colour – whether matt or shiny. When it catches reflections, it turns white like water reflecting the sky. Grey can be infinitely nuanced – shades of charcoal, elephant, dove and the delicate pearl grey of Louis Seize.

The sense of style begins in the entrance lobby, which opens discreetly off the corner of Park Lane. There is a touch of Alice in Wonderland in the outsize lampshades above the reception desk, signalling that you are entering a different world with an element of make-believe. There is wit, too, in the all-white panel of trompe l'oeil baroque windows on the wall – a tribute to the architect Sir Edwin Lutyens who had an impish humour of his own and who added distinctive flourishes to Grosvenor House, including these very windows.

Grosvenor House, completed in 1930, brought the scale of American city hotels to London, combining 800 hotel rooms with serviced flats. It replaced the London home of the Grosvenors, Dukes of Westminster, to general dismay at the leap in scale. To reduce monotony, the architect L. Rome Guthrie designed it as four stepped blocks partly connected by cross wings. The plainness of the neo-Georgian frontages did not appeal to the Grosvenor Estate and Lutyens was brought in to add architectural flair and interest. He did this in the classic skyscraper manner of 1920s New York – which he had visited for the first time in 1925 – by giving the building both a stylish base and an exotic crown, relieving any monotony in between. Above the entrances are English baroque windows with rounded tops, bottoms and keystones. This is the leitmotif found in the lobby and one that returns in the apartments above, with six-paned Georgian-style sash windows and ten-paned glazed doors onto the balcony.

Jumeira Hotels aims to serve an international clientele while drawing interest from local culture and the cities in which it locates. Hempel picks up the theme by using large panel photographs of recent London landmarks shot at striking, often vertiginous, angles. The lobby lifts take guests to a second-floor atrium of impressive proportions, rising seven storeys. The architecture

A glowing hearth is a signature of many Anouska Hempel interiors

is insistently contemporary though, with a repeating window pattern intended to create order and harmony. Instead of the usual open hotel lobby for people to mingle, the floor is treated like a sunken garden laid out with banquettes and seats as geometrical as the compartments in a Japanese breakfast tray. Look closer and the monotony of the wall treatment is broken by the pairs of louvred shutters projecting at exact right angles. The upper storey is also distinctive with alternate pillars replaced by glass.

The harmonious geometry of tables and seats in the atrium

Louvred shutters all at exact right angles to the windows echo the formality of the furniture and sunken floor

Designers everywhere are challenged by long hotel corridors and here they repeat around the atrium. Hempel's solution is to go with the grain and to turn the length to advantage by creating strongly marshalled vistas. The walls are jet black but skirtings and cornices are recessed with bands of glowing light emanating from a hidden source. Doors have metal panels like lift doors – a visual game creating surprise as they open.

The apartments vary in size but are all intended to provide the spaciousness demanded in the international market, which is often difficult to achieve in European cities. The choice begins with studio apartments facing onto the atrium. Each one offers a sense of arrival and the fun of exploring the unpredictable. Just as the appeal of traditional French hotels often lies in matching the patterns of curtains, wallpapers, upholstery and bed covers, here black bed covers are matched by black bedbacks rising to the ceiling, with bedside tables as black as lacquer and black drum lampshades.

The fashion of the 1990s and the 2000s was for ever more opulent marble hotel bathrooms. Here, there is a new chic with grey walls and grey slate. The strictest geometry prevails. Goodbye to the rounded forms of the traditional baths and basins, which have been with us since Victorian times. Instead there is the perfectionist discipline of the ruler and the set square. Line is all. The bath is generous in length with stone edging to match the walls. Carefully hidden lights illuminate the base and the edges of the glass doors, which are translucent and not hinged but pivoted.

Cupboard doors often deaden the walls of hotel rooms, so much so that some hotels now go for hanging racks. Here Hempel gives wardrobes a new sense of style with glass doors backed by her trademark handwritten indentures with their beautiful calligraphy: 'Guests love them,' I was told. On the shelf above the hanging spaces are neatly lined boxes for storage – like smart hatboxes with leather side straps.

In the apartments that overlook the atrium, total privacy can be provided by electronic blinds. On request, windows onto the atrium can be opened and the louvred outer shutters closed.

The showpieces are the penthouse apartments, which have roof terraces looking out over the roofs of Mayfair and the lofty trees of Hyde Park. These apartments are very large with three or four bedrooms, sitting and dining rooms and a cinema room. They are made all the more stylish by the use of enfilades along window walls, creating framed perspectives. Cleverly placed mirrors

Three giant black drum lampshades, three black bowls and three white Lutyens window motifs contrast with the calculated asymmetry of the reception desk and its bold cantilever

The lift lobby and corridor are lined with monochrome photographs of London's modern landmarks

Low lighting in a corridor plays up the illuminated full-length figures at the end

multiply the vistas and reflections and extend the bounds of space. The classical symmetry is picked up in the glazing bars of the sash windows – black, of course – which add a richness that modern plate glass does not provide. Pattern is emphasized by Anouska Hempel's trademark groups of pictures – many of these on strong architectural themes, including large colour photographs of the great buildings of Italy, almost the size of posters. Some are hung in pairs or double-banked, or clustered in smaller groups. In the internal corridors linking the rooms, clever use is made of small boldly framed mirrors grouped in sixes like door panels.

In the hotel room bathrooms the emphasis is on strict geometric lines as picked up with wash basins that have the vertical sides and square form of the classic sink in Edwardian pantries. As you look out of the window, it is evident that the palette of black or grey set off by brilliant orange or tangerine echoes the slate roofs and warm orangey bricks of late Victorian houses in Mayfair's streets.

The monochrome is varied in a small number of apartments, where the palette changes to black and white with half-moon sofas upholstered in white with black cushions.

Each apartment comes with a fridge, oven, sink, dishwasher and even a washer-dryer. There are electronic controls for lights, shutters and blinds, massive flat-screen TVs and very comfortable beds. It is a sci-fi world. Illuminated LEDs appear on all the wall switches, phones and controls. Many customers evidently relish this; others may need a lesson or two.

Twin hanging lamps are reflected in the
mirror panel doors, which are echoed in the
cupboards beyond. Arum lilies set in glass
tubes provide a flash of colour in contrast
to the monochrome tones

Overleaf: Black and white walls, white ceiling
and curtains with a baby grand piano set
on jigsaw-patterned pale grey carpet

In the penthouse living room, the strict
geometry of the windows, curtains, pictures
and mirrors is set off by the playful alternation of
the cushions on the sofa, which has a curving
back that descends to form comfortable arms

In the atrium reception area, the large black squares of the floor reflect the ceiling lights, which also glint in the stainless steel side tables with their cylinder tops

ANOUSKA HEMPEL

Emphatic dark lampshades create pools of light
above and below. Note the bold black frame of
the tall window looking over the atrium

Right: Clever lighting gives the mirror doors
of the cupboards a lustrous glint

ANOUSKA HEMPEL

In this bathroom the materials are all a precise match of the same subtle shade of grey. Perfect symmetry reigns with a play on squares and rectangles – twin basins, twin mirrors and sets of candles on square trays are echoed on the plinth below with the towels wrapped like a parcel

Left: The washbasin and bath are faced in matching polished black granite with a pivoting door that stands at exactly 90 degrees when open

THE INTERIOR OF THIS KNIGHTSBRIDGE HOUSE WAS RE-CREATED IN 2012 as a London home for the Weinbergs. 'Anouska and her team moved in and in six weeks the house was transformed,' Sir Mark says. 'The interior was all white and woodwork' – now it is lacquer black with lacquer used as insistently and opulently as amber was in the famous Amber Room at Tsarskoye Selo in Russia. The man who created this wealth of immaculate lacquer work is Paul Carter, Anouska Hempel's long-standing cabinetmaker and dexterous craftsman assistant, who produced lacquer screens and a large group of tables and chairs in a modern oriental mode, some pieces muscular and masculine, others graceful and feline.

This is an interior that is intended to sparkle on the greyest of days. The black front door opens into a lobby with glazed double doors leading through to a cocoon-like entrance hall aligned with the main stairs. Here a virtue is made of the typical narrow hallway of a London terraced house by decorating it as a series of distinct, telescopic sections. This clever definition of small spaces is, of course, an indirect homage to the 18th-century master of illusion and reflection in London houses, Sir John Soane.

The first half of the hallway has a shallow barrel vault lit by concealed cove lights and painted in broad alternating bands of burnished gold to give the appearance of increased width. The black livery embraces doors and doorways, dado, mirror frames and even the stacks of *FMR*, the 1980s Italian magazine, praised as the most beautiful in the world, which pioneered the all-black cover. Prints of classical urns and plants framed in black and gold complete the scene.

The front morning room has a black-topped table that is the perfect place to work with a laptop or to hold a meeting. Behind a screen is a built-in kitchen, compact and fully equipped like a galley on a yacht. Silvered screens, resembling mirrors, are overlaid in a chevron pattern.

The wooden staircase rises in one long flight to grand effect, turning back in a shorter flight to the first floor. Walls are hung with framed architectural prints. Slender column balusters are painted matt black. The staircase ends in the corner of a lofty well-proportioned first-floor dining room, square in shape and lent drama by a second staircase that strikes out in a new direction, climbing steeply up one side of the room before turning sharply to disappear through the ceiling.

Double doors lead into the front first-floor drawing room. The threshold is a rug woven in a miniature black and white chequer pattern, which is repeated in the matching stippling of the floorboards. The three tall windows are hung with black curtains in deep folds. In the centre of the room, backed by a tall screen, are twin black daybeds turned towards the windows, with full-length black mattress cushions. The chimneypiece is of blond limestone and flanked by pedestal cupboards carrying a matching pair of 18th-century Adamesque knife urns, faced with exquisite polished veneer. The walls are hung, not with pictures, but with

A knotted cord and Chinese seal make for a cushion as smart as any evening handbag

mirrors set in emphatic, vigorously moulded frames in the Dutch 17th-century manner. A pair of uplighter lamps crowned by Austrian eagles stands guard at either end of the room. An oriental note is added by cross-legged Chinese chairs and a long highly polished wooden stool with sabre legs.

The double doors between the rooms are not folded back but left open at exact right angles to the doorway. This has a broad black surround for added emphasis. Twin tables, half-enclosed by black-framed glass screens, stand on either side of the double doors with a velvet-clad chest in the centre supporting a column capped by an ormolu urn.

The house stands in Ennismore Gardens, overlooking a square shaded by immensely lofty plane trees. First reports of plans for 'a beautiful square of first-class houses' south of Hyde Park appeared in *The Builder* in April 1843. They were to be built on the twenty-one acres of an aristocratic Georgian mansion, Kingston House. In the familiar London manner, the impetus for these grand houses in what was to be Ennismore Gardens and Prince's Gate came not from the new Earl but from a Bedford carpenter's son, John Elger, who had made a fortune as a speculative builder in the South Street area of Mayfair in the 1820s and 1830s.

In the first-floor drawing room, the extensive use of black lacquer for furniture and screens makes this the most oriental of Hempel's designs. At once modern and chic, it employs traditional forms to create beautiful proportions. Seating is low but screens and lattice cupboards are tall, adding stateliness to this London terraced house interior

The first-floor drawing room looks out across the centre of the square garden. Curtains are lit by a pair of uplighters supported on the wings of Austrian eagles. A round-topped Russian table inlaid with large green marble leaves contrasts with smooth new lacquer seats

Oriental stacking food bowls form an ornamental grouping set against a black background inset with mirrors

No. 48 is part of a terrace of houses, Nos 39–59, built by Elger himself between 1849 and 1854; they quickly filled up with tenants. This was in marked contrast to the houses overlooking Hyde Park that were blighted by the construction of the Crystal Palace, which blocked the view, and sold only when it was demolished. Nos 47–59 were completed in 1852.

The houses are Italianate in style in the palazzo manner of Charles Barry and given character by grouping the windows in threes – in contrast to the treatment in Belgravia and Regent's Park, where individual houses were subsumed in a palace terrace.

Internally, the houses have been repeatedly remodelled by their fashionable owners. At No. 56, Sir William Marriott, former counsel for the ex-Khedive of Egypt, Ismail Pasha, had his drawing room redesigned in 1890 to a Moorish theme, complete with embroidered couches and draperies, arches, mirrored panels and 'yielding Turkish carpets'.

Hempel's transformation of one of these houses is at least as startling, intense and stylish. It is conceived as a journey – a rite of passage into an exotic world of the imagination and a progression from one intricately wrought space to another.

An exquisitely fashioned basket of bronzed metal flowers stands out against a filigree oriental-style screen

Black on black is the theme of this display of cases, bowls and food baskets in the morning rooms

ANOUSKA HEMPEL

The wealth of wares made for travel and household storage has long been one of Hempel's passions. In the morning room, baskets, barrels and trunks add interest to a polished black table with a black metal pyramid lampshade above

Left: A silvered globe provides a misted reflection that contrasts with that of the large bevelled mirror behind it. Right: An elegant Adamesque knife urn and a bold baroque mirror frame in the Dutch manner

The staircase ascends into the first-floor dining room with its black table surrounded by elegant, newly made black lacquer chairs with slender frames. The white cushions pick up the displays of wax seals hung on the wall of the stairs. An overhead light highlights the engraved ornament on the crystals

Opposite: Striped matting on the stairs is a match for the polished wood of the steps and snaking handrail. The banisters, in the form of slender Doric columns, are painted black to echo the walls

VADUZ HOUSE

The entrance gate opens onto a vista of mature topiary

The entrance porch with four tall Doric columns painted to look like monoliths of grey marble

'MAGNUM IN PARVO' RUNS THE LATIN TAG: GRANDEUR IN MINIATURE. In scale the Feichtingers' new house is no larger or more imposing than its neighbours, occupying the precise plot ratio of 35 per cent allowable in the well-ordered township of Vaduz. Its neighbours on Mareestrasse, which winds up the hill below the picturesque castle of the Princes of Liechtenstein, are in variations of the chalet style. The house is in the spirit of a French 18th-century *pavillon de plaisance*, a compact house built for the enjoyment of life in a country setting. Though it has close neighbours, it enjoys an exquisite view south across vineyards to the snow-capped Alps. From every window there is a leafy vista, especially beautiful when spring or autumn leaves are on the trees. 'You'll know it's Anouska Hempel as soon as you see it,' laughed Caroline Feichtinger as she gave me directions.

It is true – the topiary and the pergola loom above the road like an artist's signature. Less clear is where to park. 'Bentley Parking Only – All Others will be Crushed' says a notice on the short slipway to the garage.

A quarter circle of steps leads up to the front gate, the ends gently disappearing into the cobbled pavement. The gate, like so much that follows, is handsomely cast in lead, always the ultimate material for smart garden features. It opens onto a path paved with grey stone setts. To the right is a raised terrace with a trim pergola of plane trees, each one perfectly straight with the branches pleached to form a level canopy, which requires trimming at least three times a year.

The question is whether to continue straight to the inviting garden terrace that looks out across the valley, or to walk round the flank of the house hoping to find a front entrance. The mighty twin-columned portal that comes into view is worthy of standing guard at the Bank of Switzerland. The smooth grey column shafts look like monoliths cut from the living rock but are in fact stone painted to resemble seamless grey marble.

As the 3.6-metre-high double doors open, the sense of theatricality is all-enveloping. You step into a modern staircase hall in stunning shades of grey, worthy of comparison with the 18th-century baroque staircases – *treppenhauser* – of central European palaces and summer houses. This may be smaller than many but it is a marvel of engineering and artistry, the more enchanting for its domestic scale.

To understand the concept of the house as a progression from dark to light, night to day, I am told I must descend to the lower floor first. Here, in the basement, is the grand entrance for cars, a large columnless exhibition gallery for the prize items in Dr Feichtinger's collection. These include an Aston Martin Cygnet, one of a limited edition, and a 1956 Porsche 550 RS Spyder, in which Dr Feichtinger has lapped the great circuits of Europe. On the walls are black-framed mirrors, providing multiple reflections of the stylish cars. In the corner is a discreet work-out area.

Entering the staircase hall, the floor is laid in the same grey slate as the staircase. To the left, a door opens into a spacious laundry room with extra-large Belfast sinks and a splendid wooden-topped worktable. Another door reveals a wine cellar stacked high with crates of first-growth clarets. 'My husband says life is too short to drink bad wine,' says Caroline Feichtinger.

The staircase rises in twin curving flights around the walls with a glinting bronze handrail and a black iron balustrade. The balusters are slender, continuing in an unbroken run to the top of the house without a single newel post. Lateral strength is provided by an X-pattern border that binds each baluster with its neighbours. This is a leitmotif – its inspiration will emerge later. Arriving on the main level, the matching black floor is laid in a bold pattern of large squares of black slate edged in oak to form a bold diamond parquet. This continues as a unifying theme through every room including the kitchen – without the thresholds one finds in doorways in earlier centuries.

The walls of the staircase hall are painted to simulate blocked masonry – the traditional French treatment for an entrance hall. But the wall opposite the entrance is subtly different, much silkier and without the stone blocking. The chimneypiece carved in jet black stone is a double conceit. It is the twin of the outdoor fireplace facing the front door – a yin and yang relationship in which each is the mirror image of the other, one indoors, one outdoors. The fireplace has no back but also opens into the salon beyond, guarded from throwing sparks by sliding glass shutters on both sides.

Mountains rise steeply behind the house

The house has the compact form of an 18th-century Trianon

A pretty painted fillet adorns a door frame

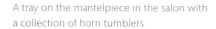
A tray on the mantelpiece in the salon with a collection of horn tumblers

On either side of the staircase hall, doors open into the main salon, which has three tall French windows opening into the garden. The colour scheme is Hempel's favourite black and tan. The walls are lined with jet black silk while the curtains hang in thick folds of dark grey shot silk, glinting in the light from the windows. The fabric is boldly bunched at the top and spills over the floor like the train of a ballgown. Over the fireplace a tall Empire mirror is lit by three downlighters that create sparkling refractions in the cut-glass borders. In the corners by the windows are two matching round tables, one with a brown suede cloth, the other in matt black. Flanking the fire are a pair of dark grey kid leather sofas with serpentine backs in best Chippendale manner, each with a tan cushion providing an accent. The sofas are enclosed by tall glazed screens overhung with miniature lattices with black lacquer frames, a deliberately oriental touch.

Over the round tables are low-hanging, square metal lampshades with sloping slides like a hipped roof, black without and bronze within. This is part of Hempel's continuous play with varied geometric forms. Another amusing touch is a petite drum-shaped chair – for once only a single – covered in soft, tan-coloured leather.

The salon's walls are hung with two floor-to-ceiling engravings of Roman victory columns while the doors at the ends of the room are flanked with slender baroque mirrors. Every surface is an opportunity for a tableau or display of a collection of charming or unusual objects – for example the drinking horns on the mantle shelf.

On the left of the salon, double doors open into a kitchen panelled in blond pine in the Austrian chalet fashion. Nonetheless, this is a super-chic modern version with jet black surfaces setting off the warm pine. The large dining table is a single smooth slab of Welsh slate with a border of pine, and a splendid chandelier formed of intertwined deer antlers hangs low over it. All the working surfaces are of polished black granite.

The longer window wall has a striking built-in centrepiece: a chest dresser with central cupboards surrounded by tiers of small drawers for spices and herbs, which is modelled on an oriental one at Cole Park. Dr Feichtinger is a keen cook and, for intimate suppers, likes his guests to sit at this table while he cooks. Beyond is a smaller inner kitchen where dishes can go to be washed and where an assistant can operate discreetly in the background.

Between the two kitchens is a pair of unusual antique windows, which caught the Feichtingers' attention at Guinevere Antiques in Holland. They are inset with X-pattern glazing bars, which provided a leitmotif for the interior of the house. In the kitchen they are echoed in the back of the elegant low-backed oak benches supplied for the dining table.

The pine panelling is given a distinctive touch with short Corinthian pilasters with basket capitals. On top of the dresser is a row of wine decanters of unusual baroque shapes matched by extra-large, tall-stemmed wine glasses on the window ledges, an allusion to the libations that will flow and the equivalent of the bunches of grapes and vine leaves used in 18th-century dining rooms on ceilings and chimneypieces.

Light flows into the staircase hall through 3.6-metre-tall double doors, illuminating the sweeping double staircase and the giant twin lanterns, hanging low, to emphasize the generous scale

The fireplace in the hall is also open to the room beyond, while the globe mirror above reflects the outdoor fireplace facing the front door

Twin leather armchairs in the study match the colour of the walls

On the far side of the salon is the library with large twin writing desks for the owners. The windows have concertina-style shutters. The tall narrow folds are inset with mirror panels to create evening reflections. Clever use is made of spotlights and lampshades to provide pools of light and to highlight individual elements. Dr Feichtinger says, 'When we have a big dinner party here we take out the desks and bring in little theatre chairs so we can sit sixteen.' His favourite chefs are Andrea Caminada, 'the best in Switzerland', who has cooked here on special occasions, and Neville Campbell, who worked at Blakes.

Returning to the staircase hall, the impressive height of the two-storey space is apparent. The staircase rises as an 'Imperial' – two matching flights hugging the walls until they unite and leap across space to the first-floor landing. In 18th-century England the game was to make these cantilever stairs ever leaner and more elegant, cutting away the undersides of the stone treads. Here a different, baroque aesthetic is at work and the powerful curves are emphasized by the broad base, which carries the balustrade. By contrast the balustrade is Neo-classical in inspiration. Both harmonize in an uninterrupted curve sweeping up and down. The window walls are stepped forward to provide pedestals for rows of five perfectly matched urns. Carefully controlled daylight streams in through three *oeil-de-boeufs* – bull's-eye windows – set high in the wall. At the upper level, the paler grey on the side walls is enlivened by groups of painted frames edged in black and arranged in three rows of three. This is another of Hempel's

inventions – the use of emphatic but empty picture frames to create the effect of wall panelling.

Precision geometry and engineering are evident in the way that the individual steps fan out almost like playing cards, each at an angle to the last, as the staircase curves upwards. In a final bravura flourish the continuous bronze handrails do not end in a newel post but descend at right angles straight into the landing.

Here, the palette changes. The first floor is paved throughout in large polished squares of pure white Carrara marble, set in the same diamond pattern as the black slate below. The three rooms at the front, looking over the valley, form a suite with a bedroom in the centre. Caroline Feichtinger's dressing room to the left is balanced by a bathroom to the right. Tall windows provide lovely views in every direction. The inspiration, says Caroline Feichtinger, was the Corfu Suite at Blakes – all white and beige – her favourite. A new flourish is added with mother-of-pearl inlay in a spangled pattern on the American white oak bedposts and finials. It is a tour de force created by Paul Carter to Hempel's design. Some nine thousand pieces of inlay are set by hand into tapered grooves. The bed curtains are of ivory-white ribbed satin lined with an icing-sugar white silk, also used for the dome above the bed, which rises in a gentle serpentine curve from the four corners. The large dressing table is another masterpiece by Carter. One of the glass panels on top lifts up to reveal a triptych mirror that glides up, perfectly balanced by lead counterweights.

The double staircase rises from the basement and continues to the bedrooms

In the salon, the black and tan livery of the cushions and leather armchair is picked up by the handsome striped trunk serving as a coffee table

The upper landing leads on either side to matching bedrooms for the Feichtingers' two daughters. They have chosen the colours – one blue, one caramel – and each has a four-poster bed with striped barbers' pole columns. In both, a staircase leads up to a bathroom neatly inserted beneath the sloping eaves and lit by a bull's-eye window. The baths look out through the window and the basins are set in polished Portuguese limestone, which is carried over to the baths, set at right angles to provide a satisfying geometry. The bathroom stairs also open into a large square playroom beneath the centre of the roof. Sturdy roof beams are exposed to view and have been painted a chalky white to lighten the space.

Satin curtains glisten in the strong Alpine light

With snow lying outside for several months each year, there are limits to what can be grown in the garden, but this does not a restrict Hempel, who likes to work with a palette of lawns and evergreens. French windows open out onto a stone-paved terrace set with a pair of matching dining tables each made with two vast slabs of Welsh slate. The lawn below is edged with a pair of vine pergolas, framing the view across the vineyard to the mountains.

The outdoor swimming pool adds the final flourish. 'In the mountains it's not appropriate to have a turquoise pool as in the south of France,' says Caroline Feichtinger. The pool is faced in flame-finished black granite. It is long and quite narrow, intended for exercise. The water spills over the sides, animating the polished black marble facing. The levels are so perfectly calculated that the water ceases to spill over at exactly the point where the sides of the pool begin to disappear into the slope of the hill. All the trees and shrubs come from the designer's favourite nursery in Hamburg, which supplies mature and perfectly matched trees.

The interior of the house was created in a similar fashion, with a kit of parts sent from England and Hempel's chosen craftsmen and artisans arriving in relays to fit out, decorate, furnish and finish it. The house is laid out – carport apart – to a strictly geometric and symmetrical plan.

The completion of this house as a perfect classical villa in a distinctly contemporary idiom is unquestionably a triumph for Anouska Hempel and her whole team. It is conceived and furnished as a complete work of art – a *Gesamtkunstwerk* as the German art historians say – yet it is also a supremely luxurious and comfortable home tailored to the owners' needs. There is certainly no other practice in Britain, and few elsewhere in the world, that could produce such a sophisticated combination of interiors, architecture and gardens so superbly finished, using fine materials and craftsmanship, to such good effect. The Feichtingers' house is at once a well-tuned machine for living in (to adapt Corbusier's famous phrase) but also a delight to guests and visitors. More than that, it is a reaffirmation of the sparkling brilliance to which the decorative arts can aspire.

The downstairs cloakroom is a play on black and gold

Opposite: The salon is divided by glazed screens in black frames overhung with matching lattice panels. The floor is laid in a diamond pattern with large squares of Welsh slate set in oak borders

The kitchen is fitted in blond Austrian pine with built-in dressers and polished black granite worktops. The large oven is French and the low-backed benches around the dining table are in oak

The handrail descends in a continuous sweep supported by slender metal balusters

The house is conceived as a progression from dark to light, with a luminous ivory-white main bedroom suite. The floor is laid with large squares of white Carrara marble set in a diamond pattern. The same satin fabric is used for the window and bed curtains. The four-poster bed is inlaid with mother-of-pearl to match the favourite chest of the owners

In the all-white guest bedroom, white bed curtains are complemented by white porcelain and seating

Twin garden tables made of large slabs of Welsh slate stand on the garden terrace, shaded in the summer by umbrellas

Tall glazed French windows open onto the garden terrace with mirrored shutters behind

The terrace by the entrance is raised on a low plinth with a garden table flanked by low-backed oak benches. The pergola is formed of pleached plane trees providing dappled shade

The swimming pool provides a mirror image of twin garden benches flanked by striped pots filled with topiary spheres. Below: Two views of the entrance gate show the lead panels used to provide a super-smart facing to low garden walls

THIS IS A HOUSE THAT LIVES ABOVE ALL AT NIGHT, WHEN SPARKLING candlelight is reflected in countless mirrors and glass lamps. For Anouska Hempel these features are equally a means of shutting out dank London weather. As noted earlier, she finds grey skies unbearable, having grown up in the bright sun of the southern hemisphere. Her solution is to fill the garden outside the windows with plants that stay fresh and green throughout the year – box, yew, laurel, camellias, magnolia – and then to blank out the sky by pulling blinds down over the tops of the windows.

Inside the Weinbergs' home, where they lived until 2012, everything is the opposite of the typical London town house, just as a black and white negative is the exact reverse of the photographic print made from it. Elements that are usually light and bright are dark, in shades ranging from ebony and inky black to slate greys and deep greens. The dark tones give the interior a sense of unfolding mystery. Doors may have vanished from their hinges and one room flows into the next. The boundaries between them are scarcely apparent and judiciously placed mirrors create a sense of infinite recession. Yet in the positioning of furniture there is an strict logic. These are places permanently ready for guests at any time of day or evening. At the end of the drawing room, a table is constantly laid ready for a smart oriental breakfast.

'I have a grasshopper mind,' Hempel says disarmingly. Yet her concentration is total. Her thoughts and visual imagination are constantly racing: words cannot keep up with thoughts, and ideas and designs take form without need for language. 'I have frog's eyes. I can scan a room and take in everything in it,' she continues. Her visual memory extends not only to objects, fabrics and colours, but also to decorative techniques and effects she has observed on her travels. Though Hempel's tastes are eclectic, combining styles and features from different countries, continents and periods, the interiors are never copies or reincarnations, but new creations in which ideas and themes are developed, often obsessively. It works thanks to a lightness of touch mixed with an engaging sense of fun.

Her commitment to 'layering' in her interiors often results in several dimensions: sometimes a physical overlay creates an added sense of richness; sometimes one culture is overlaid with another. Her approach is not based on a strict ideology like Modernism or a set of rules and proportions like Classicism. It is born instead of an extraordinary sense for forming groups of objects and creating vistas, matched by a confidence and determination to get the desired result, however much trouble it takes.

A second element is her enthusiasm, bordering on mania, for shopping. Again it is the sheer range of things that catch her eye that is remarkable. They include not only precious, highly wrought objets d'art and expensive fabrics, but also simple, everyday items produced for local consumption. Her shopping

A thick magnolia hedge above the garden wall creates privacy

extends beyond visits to fashionable emporia and smart design outlets, to include trips to antique shops and street-market stalls. Her eye for decorative objects as much as for fine art adds an exotic element to her interiors. With this goes an unceasing delight in stylish packaging of all ages and places – boxes, jars, urns, vessels, containers of every kind. As noted earlier, she rarely buys single objects. She is always on the lookout for pairs, threesomes or even a dozen of any exotic item that appeals.

She talks of the 'architecture of everything I do'. If architecture is considered an art as opposed to a profession, she is certainly an architect in her approach, not sitting at the drawing board with a set square, but ever ready with her ball of string to lay out a line. She possesses a rare, in-built spirit level (helped occasionally by the real thing) to ensure that no picture frame is ever hanging at an angle and that every hedge top is evenly clipped. The final crucial element comes with the craftsmen she regularly employs. With them she evolves a design, occasionally with the help of a rough sketch but often simply through discussion.

'I travel to Salzburg and Turkey and New York taking my team with me. I have a wealth of talent. My cabinetmakers deserve recognition as much as David

Ordered, symmetrical planting not only frames the front door with enticing result but also has the effect of setting the house further away from the road

Intricate detailing invigorates the tight space of the entrance hall. Note the spear balustrade below the stairs and the multiple reflections on the walls and floor

Lindley,' she enthuses. While some interior designers are unwilling to name the specialist artists and craftsmen they work with for fear that rivals might poach them, she is very keen that her collaborators should have credit and recognition. What she will not accept is for her collaborators to take her ideas to other clients of their own. 'If they are working for someone else they must produce their own ideas not mine,' she says firmly.

'I can get the best out of people, make them feel good about themselves. It works if they can stand the pressure. People get excited by the pace. There is an electric feel in the air. I can't bear committees. I am a team player, with my own team.' With such determined ideas, one of Hempel's main challenges has been to find a way of negotiating with planning officials. 'When I walked into Addison Road I was confronted by a wall. It had to go. I'll never take no for an answer. I'll fight all the way.' She adds, ' But the key in discussions is to make the other chap feel good about what he is telling you. You don't put anyone down.'

Addison Road takes the desire to create total effects into a new sphere. It follows on from the art nouveau interiors of the early 1900s when architects favoured the *tout ensemble*, designing every element of the interior down to the carpets, wallpapers and coat hooks. These interiors were a sensation when they first appeared in Brussels, Paris and Vienna. Yet they were also a short-lived phenomenon, a fireworks display that burnt itself out in ten years, partly because it was so overwhelming and extreme and such a straightjacket to live in.

Hempel is driven by the same desire to marshal every decorative element into a single artistic composition. Her designs succeed, however, where earlier designs failed, because this overwhelming conviction comes with a love of entertaining, spoiling and surprising guests. Nor are the furnishings frozen forever in one position. This is a magician's box of tricks, which in a trice can be reconfigured and rearranged, judiciously weeded or embellished as impulse dictates. Shades of colour are chosen and matched with care so there is never a jarring note. There is always an element of mystery, more to look at than is immediately apparent.

The main staircase at Addison Road was transformed by the introduction of a series of polished steel balusters that are carried up like spears beyond the handrail and set diamond-wise on the treads. In the drawing room beyond, one space merges into another but furniture is placed with such precision that it might all have been drawn out on graph paper. The arrangement revolves round formal groups of seats. Hempel has no time for lolling on sofas or sinking into deep cushions. 'I like to sit upright,' she says, echoing the French belief that conversation will be brighter if people sit on upright chairs. The floor is in Italian green marble. The white veining disturbed her and every last trace was carefully chipped out with a chisel. 'I start with the floor. The design of a room is set by the floor,' she says. The floor provides the cue for the deep green of the walls. 'It's a green like that of rising damp in Venice,' she continues.

Her method usually is to work in just two colours. Here, the second colour is provided by the doors, made of solid Brazilian mahogany. 'It's an idea I copied from the Bank of England and the Soane Museum,' she explains. The big scale

is deliberate, as is the attention to detail. One pair of doors has projecting 'Parliament' hinges that allow them to fold right back against the wall. Another is without hinges and swings on a pivot so that it can open in both directions. 'If I am having a big dinner I like to be able to close doors to make secluded areas for people to chat,' she says.

The blinds that shut out the grey skies are her trademark durries from India, which are here painted in grey and russet stripes. The window frames and glazing bars are painted in charcoal grey to match the walls – intensifying the brilliance of the green leaves outside. On the sills of windows, delicate white orchids add a further accent. In front of two windows stand elegant iron benches with backs forming interlacing figures of eight. The seat cushions are in a pretty grey-blue watered silk, with additional neat stacks of striped cushions placed at intervals, four to each pile. On warm summer evenings, a different mood is created when the continuous windows onto the garden are folded back to give an almost tropical openness.

Over the dining table is a cluster of glass globe lights suspended from a striped turban. These are matched by a series of glass bells, hanging from a

Above: Sunlight floods through the hall from the garden. Below: A classic example of layering with clusters of objects and subtle reflections

Lattice blinds and screens, complemented by artfully placed mirrors, make it hard to distinguish windows from reflections. Overleaf: Fan lights and French windows bring the richly planted garden indoors on a warm day, though a sense of shade, cool and restfulness is created by the darker tones within. The floor reflects the sunlight on the leaves of the trees and sky above

ANOUSKA HEMPEL

bamboo frame in front of the bay window: 'Smoke catchers used in Oxford and Cambridge to catch cigar smoke,' she explains. The bay window at the end of the room is largely concealed by a screen of folding mirrors – tall and thin with shaped, baroque tops. These reappear throughout the house, always formed of three or six folds. Pointing to a pair of glass-fronted cases with lattice-pattern doors she adds, 'I am very fond of Irish proportions. There are all sorts of things about their furniture which are not quite conventional, which gives them a special appeal.'

Hempel has a talent for making small spaces as much an event as large salons. This begins with the downstairs cloakroom, an essay in jet black with mirror panels reflecting the black woodwork. Though there is more mirror than wall, the tonality remains uncannily black, an effect multiplied by the black marble around the basin. The kitchen is given warmth and elegance by the pale figured birchwood used for the cupboards above and below the black worktops. The cupboard doors have black borders in the manner of ebony inlay on antique furniture, as well as smart black button handles.

The adjoining small breakfast room is a cabinet of curiosities that would have delighted a 17th-century collector. Along the mantelshelf is a line of ivory cricket cases that she has collected. 'Elegant Chinese ladies put these in the sleeves of their kimonos. You could tell their status by the sound of the cricket singing,' she explains. On the two bamboo stands on either side of the fireplace is a collection of boxes made of porcupine quills as well as pairs of ivory truffle scrapers. By the door to the kitchen there are framed groups of wax seals, made up to Hempel's order and set against a background of elegantly lettered indentures. The boarded floor is painted in imitation of a diamond parquetry of light and dark woods surrounded by her trademark rope border. It contrasts with the slate grey walls and black marble surround to the fireplace.

A lunette window folds down to create an unusual porthole

Below left: Twin lunettes create a binocular view into the garden. Below right: A bronze head of a sphinx in glancing light

In a darkened room, reflections play tricks with the eye

One bedroom has still richer treatment, with mirrored cupboard doors framed by borders of boulle work inset with patterned brass and tortoiseshell. Picture frames are as elaborate as the prints within. A set of five red lacquer Chinese pots on a console table is doubled in number by its reflection in the mirror behind. Another trademark, table lamps with slender bamboo stems are topped by shades like Chinese coolie hats. A group is ranged against the leaded window in a bathroom. Other details that could all too easily be missed are the ghostly trompe l'oeil columns with scrolled Ionic capitals looming above framed prints that hang on the walls.

The master bedroom is as crowded with treasures as an ancient Egyptian tomb chamber. The curtains, with narrow horizontal stripes, even take their cue

from the famous blue and gold striped headdress of the boy king Tutankhamun. The colour scheme is taken up by the piles of cushions, diminishing in size, first beige then blue, while tall mirror panels on the cupboards create reflections, with an added glint provided by brass edgings. Everywhere imaginative flourishes stand out, such as a black and gold gadrooned frame and the bands of black and gold beading in the cornice. 'I love trunks, boxes and drawers stuffed with goodies,' she laughs.

The windows of the first-floor rooms look out on a beautifully ordered composition of neatly clipped shrubs and carefully arranged pots that remain green in all seasons. 'I like green on green on green,' she says. In the garden itself there is the same sense of enclosure, of a private Elysium secluded from the city outside. There is not a corner that has not been subject to her imaginative and disciplined eye. Spreading lawns offer calmness and repose, while terraces and paths are an invitation to explore and seek out every vista.

Numerous fine stuccoed houses in Belgravia, Knightsbridge and Kensington now have elegant terracotta pots filled with carefully clipped spheres of box crowding front gardens, porches and balconies. It all began at Addison Road where Anouska Hempel's smart paving and pots, glimpsed through a gate in the high wall, have been heralding a temple of design for well over a decade.

Dazzling symmetry created with tumblers, decanters and coasters all chosen for their strong clean lines

To adapt four well-known lines of an English hymn: 'A man that looks on glass, On it may stay his eye, Or if he pleases through it pass, And then the garden espy'

Window blinds in the drawing room are lowered to the level where they shut out any glimpse
of grey English skies

Overleaf: This darkened room, with its careful highlights, echoes the cabinets of curiosities of
17th- and 18th-century collectors – small-scale intimate spaces crowded with pictures and objects.
The complexity is heightened by one of Hempel's trademark screens placed in an alcove with folds
angled to set up intriguing reflections

ANOUSKA HEMPEL

Thanks to an inexhaustible commitment to detail, every table stands ready for guests

Right: An Austrian eagle uplighter

At dusk the muted but rich colours of the
window blinds in the drawing room come
into play, while the high polish on the floor
momentarily reflects the evening sky

Concealed lighting and a live fire pick out perfectly symmetrical elements, as well as the subtle match of cushions and marble floors

In a corner of the drawing room one object
echoes another, framing a group of mirrors
arranged to look like panelling

Contrasting textures add interest with the high polish on the twin doors, the wool fabric on the walls and the shimmer of the silk cushions

In the Pudding Room, a dark band of fabric laid
with matching shallow bowls creates a strong
axis down the table. Glass globes glow with
reflected light in the otherwise darkened space

Overleaf: A group of lamps adds drama to the
fine tracery of the windows

ANOUSKA HEMPEL

Above and right: White porcelain and fresh linen are the key notes in a table arrangement with plate settings carefully ordered in trays. Below: Clever lighting picks out the minute detail on the glass

Screens are used to create a sense of enclosure
and cosiness as well as an element of mystery,
concealing what lies beyond. As always, mirrors
provide a variety of reflections

A highly polished leather trunk, baskets and
wooden cups and cylinders show how luggage
and well-made household goods can look as
handsome as fine furniture

Symmetry is absolute in this view through to a dining table with paired windows on either side of the solid wall, which blocks the vista. The blinds on the double doors are echoed in the blinds on the walls, used here as a decorative motif. White plaster paterae are arranged in glazed box frames and fill every piece of spare wall space, hung in vertical rows of six. Note the ebony black inlay in the lower doors and door frames

Framed plaster paterae on a background of old indentures are hung either side of the doors

ANOUSKA HEMPEL

Sabre-legged chairs are a perfect colour match, not only for the table but also for the tall chest of drawers between the windows and the painted geometrical floor. Striped curtains and cushions, the colour of tiger skin, add a further exotic note. The fabric is bunched at the top to resemble a row of turbans

Only the different reflections in the mirrors
either side of the fireplace artfully disturb the
perfect symmetry of this composition

An Elizabethan portrait of a lady dressed in glowing amber finds the
perfect colour match in golden cushions and highly polished veneer

Left: Clusters of
pots are arranged
to lively effect, with
drinking cups in
descending order of
height and a trio of
pear-shaped candles

Right: A row of
Chinese gourds,
each made to hold
a cricket that would
sing to its owner

The warp and weft of fabrics, woods, veneers
and carefully placed objects in the master
bedroom create a still life in the manner
of a 17th-century vanitas painting

Above: The art of a vanishing point is evident in this precisely symmetrical composition focused on a single bar of light
Right: Mirrored cupboard doors frame the looking-glass door of this cabinet, with every key hung with a matching tassel

Highly polished leather trunks have the sheen of antique furniture

Contrasting styles of four-poster beds feature in the bedrooms. Here, shades of white and beige create a feeling of intense freshness, which is accentuated by white cloths on the bedside tables and the white lampshades

Opposite: Red lacquer pots of strong geometric form add to the blaze of colour provided by the bed fabrics and walls. The painted floor is covered by a rug. Oriental travel chests suggest the exotic destinations Hempel loves. The sculpted baroque outline of the bed curtains and valances adds extra richness

Overleaf: Bamboo furniture provides a strong geometry while filigree screens veil windows and walls, creating a deep sense of privacy and intimacy. Gathered curtains add a voluptuous note and the fabric is repeated on the bedside tables to complete the *tout ensemble*. The oriental mood is picked up in the matting used as a valance on the four-poster bed

ANOUSKA HEMPEL

Above: Black louvred doors reflect the light from the garden

Left: Topiary creates luxuriance as well as a pleasing formality

Opposite: The axis of the path is picked up on the far side of the lawn by a large urn

Overleaf: Hempel's favourite clipped mushroom box trees form a conversation piece on the lawn. The house itself virtually disappears behind a green wall of trailing greenery. Pots come in a multitude of shapes and sizes, all colour coordinated

ANOUSKA HEMPEL

In contrast to the usual fanlight, the glazing of the arched windows forms a hoop

The central axis is closed by a pedestal carrying a slender obelisk

The swimming pool has a Moorish air and is shaped like a fountain pool at the Alhambra in Spain. Tiles, weathered by years in southern climes, form a perfect colour match to the walls. Oriental seats add a pretty, ornamental touch, complemented by the richly textured towel baskets, rectangular in shape like everything except the dome and arched windows. Leaves in the garden create shadow patterns on the walls

Hempel likes a garden to remain green all the
year round, hence the choice of plants, shrubs
and trees that do not lose their leaves

ANOUSKA HEMPEL

Clipped box mushrooms are used to delightful effect in numerous ways. They are grouped in picturesque clusters that frame vistas and lawns, while around the garden table (below) they are placed symmetrically

HENRY COTTON WAS AN ARCHETYPAL BRITISH SPORTING HERO. Banned from the cricket team at Dulwich College after a dispute with the headmaster, Cotton turned to golf. Winning the Hutchings Trophy aged sixteen, he embarked on a career as a professional golfer and went on to win the Open Championship three times. According to the *Oxford Dictionary of National Biography*, 'When Cotton entered his profession, the status of golf professional was barely above that of a senior caddy. By personal example Cotton did more than anyone of his time to alter that. He sought the best: silk shirts from Jermyn Street, limousines rather than taxis, and the best restaurants.'

In the Second World War Cotton enlisted with the Royal Air Force and raised money for the Red Cross in exhibition matches that earned him an MBE. He saw the need to challenge American supremacy in his sport and was a member of four British Ryder teams and the captain of two. After retiring from professional golf he became an architect of golf courses, and on the Algarve created the Penina golf course from a swamp. He wrote books and established the Golf Foundation, which helped thousands of young people to learn the game. He was knighted in the 1988 New Year's Honours but died before he could attend the ceremony at Buckingham Palace. However, as he had already accepted the knighthood it was awarded posthumously.

Henry Cotton's, the brand, had been created in 1978 to combine the lifestyle of an English country gentleman with the quality of Italian tailoring. Today

Concertina screens tailored to match a shop that is laid out in the round

the sporting aspects still dominate, with overtones of Oxford, Cambridge and Harvard. In the clothes and in the stores there is a strong element of tradition together with the most innovative materials for sporting clothes and equipment.

Henry Cotton's in Milan's fashionable Corso Venezia is a flagship store, conceived as a window onto a way of life, indeed, an induction to it, or a home from home if you are returning to it. In a theatrical and amusing way it is filled with props that recall sports of every kind, ranging from golf and rugby football to mountaineering.

Anouska Hempel designed the store around a circular stairwell inset with a lift and it unfolds as a journey of exploration from floor to floor. With a careful eye you can learn as much about the history of sport and good living as about stylish clothing for the outdoor life.

The stairwell already existed but all the components of the fit-out – shelves, wardrobes and display cases – were delivered as a kit from England and installed and finished by a team sent from Anouska Hempel Design. In Milan, famed capital of fashion, surrounded by the most clothes-conscious and best-dressed people in the world, this was no mean feat.

A bridge corridor shaped like an upturned boat seems to rest on pebbles, as if it is standing on the beach

The staircase rises from the entrance lobby and continues upwards from the first floor

The pair of window arches on the street barely hint at the Aladdin's cave of treasures within. As in a smart hotel, you first see a cloakroom where you are invited to leave your coat and bag allowing you to explore freely. The staircase winds up in a continuous curve. The colour scheme is the favourite Hempel black and tan, here in the form of simulated throws over the solid balustrade – jet black with a tan border. The handrail is wound, basket-style with raffia. 'The man came with a continuous roll winding it round for several days,' says Marcella Baraldi, the manager of the store. The stair walls are faced in a veneer of textured blond stone with matching mortar that gives an outdoorsy feel. This contrasts with the darkened spotlit spaces that create an all-enveloping world for the display of clothes.

The leitmotif on the first floor is the oar. Dozens of highly polished oars for racing eights are suspended on a rail like a movable screen or set dramatically over the staircase like a portcullis. The circular layout has prompted the creation of a series of window niches or compartments, each a tableau of sporting and travel gear: trunks, racquets, leather footballs, whitened cricket pads, fencing masks. There is a stack of heavy folio volumes, unbound in the French manner, as well as ottomans in snakeskin and a stand of fishing rods.

The standard square recesses for stacking shirts and jumpers are here turned into ebony-black library bookcases overhung by a ladder as if to reach the upper shelves. The conceit is that it is not a ladder but a sliding glazed door with

Above: Boxing paraphernalia hangs in the lift
Opposite: Giant oars stand beside the staircase

This ship model is one of many allusions to a whole range of fashionable sports

bevelled glass. Other props include old-fashioned shoe trees, of both metal and polished wood, and several classic varieties of vintage portable radios in Bakelite and leather. The walls are painted in dark colours with a dado frieze of classic JAK cartoons from the *Daily Express* newspaper.

The men's department is extended by a covered bridge into an adjoining building. It is designed to give the cocoon-like feeling of an upturned boat with wooden siding. Beach pebbles strewn beside the central gangway complete the sense of a rite of passage and halfway along is a large, well-worn leather golf-club bag, packed with drivers, not an iron in sight.

The bridge opens into a display gallery with the atmosphere of a fashionable gentleman's lair. A sense of style and raffishness is provided by a highly polished black ebonized baby grand piano with a recumbent figure on top. To the right is a handsome chimneypiece flanked by tall, narrow, glass-fronted cupboards with numbered shelves. They are designed to convey the feel of cigar thermidors complete with bundles of cigars. A standard lamp made of entwined antlers stands beside the piano.

Further along the gallery are hanging recesses for clothes with sides upholstered in smart black and white striped fabric. The lights are the familiar coolie shades with chrome arms extending from slender chrome poles to provide maximum flexibility. Free-standing glass-topped display cases are edged with stainless steel and set on stands like silver trunks.

Ascending to the second floor, the ladies department, there is the same jet-black floor and armoires with bevelled glass. Here the outer walls are faced with beautifully lettered property indentures, alternating with bold 19th-century coloured architectural prints of landmarks, such as the Pantheon in Rome and the Villa la Rotonda outside Vicenza. Shelves are upholstered in leather with neat rows of miniature brass studs. One amusing touch is a pair of lamps made from highly polished ladies' boot trees.

The changing rooms are like ingenious shower cubicles with smart black and white striped cushions. The walls are hung with a group of 'dress' sporrans from Scotland, made with fur and silver trimming. Most exotic of all are two low travelling chests that open up as ladies' dressing tables, complete with three-fold mirrors. The sides fold back to reveal little chests of drawers between which you can sit in front of the mirror. Marcella Baraldi points to a lamp admired by all: a streamlined silvered art deco table light that has the proportions of a perfect sphere but consists only of the shallow top and slender curving arm connecting it to the base.

The final flourish appears as the drum-shaped lift arrives to collect you. On the roof is a tableau of brown leather soccer and rugby footballs, while inside a cluster of leather boxing gloves hangs from the ceiling.

In an age of minimalism, it is refreshing to see objects and collectibles of so many kinds formed into amusing groups and intriguing still lifes, showing that what might be dismissed as bric-a-brac can make a contribution to creative design and a sense of both history and exploration.

Brightly lit clothes stand out invitingly from the dark floors and walls

Bare stone walls, the colour of Cotswold stone, create a masculine ambience matched by the wood and leather used for the alcoves

ANOUSKA HEMPEL

Framing the lift shaft, a pair of highly polished giant oars is a perfect match for the folding panelling

The black and tan livery
of the woodwork

Above left: A collection
of sporrans enlivens a
changing room

Above: One of a pair of
folding travelling chests
with a three-fold mirror

Left: Travel and sport are
prevailing themes

ANOUSKA HEMPEL

Above: Racing oars form a leitmotif throughout the store, here suspended from a running rail

Right: On the first floor oars serve as dividers between displays in the alcoves

HOTEL PIERRE APARTMENT   CADENCES IN BLACK AND WHITE

THERE IS NOT MUCH BETTER THAN AN APARTMENT LOOKING DOWN on the green copper and slate roof of New York's famed Plaza Hotel, complete with a panorama across Central Park. So when Anouska Hempel was asked by a Swedish businessman to design an apartment at the top of The Pierre, the renowned art deco hotel on Fifth Avenue and East 61st Street, she seized the opportunity to produce a design worthy of a place where renowned chef Auguste Escoffier prepared the dinner for the opening gala in 1930.

The eagle's eyrie apartment at the top of The Pierre looks down on the mighty 1907 Plaza Hotel on the edge of Central Park

262   ANOUSKA HEMPEL

The interior of the apartment is an electrifyingly beautiful essay in black and white and is a seismic example of Hempel's ability to create multiple variations on a theme. Order and discipline rule supreme with her trademark geometry at its most exacting and satisfying. But it is not a one-liner restricted by a monochrome palette, rather it is full of surprise and the kind of cleverness that makes you exclaim with delight.

The palette is varied by the use of pattern and numerous subtle gradations, which sit together in perfect harmony. In the living room there are shades of grey and silver. Stripes comes in all sorts and sizes: narrow black and white sideways stripes on the walls, chequered grey upholstery on the chairs and seats, overlaid with pairs of dashing black and white ribbons like go-faster stripes on a car. Large silver and black cushions in diagonal stripes sit on cushions with straight stripes that are a tad broader and more emphatic.

On the chairs, pairs of cushions match the walls rather than the upholstery. Everywhere there is a doubling up. Depth is provided by a few carefully chosen antiques – Russian hanging lamps, an 1890 portrait of two boys by Giovanni Boldini (the Italian painter who worked in London and Paris) and a 1790 German chest. Tall stick lights have black shafts matching the ribbon stripes.

In the dining room, warm highly polished mahogany is brought into play. Twin-panelled mahogany doors, positioned at exact right angles to the threshold, are echoed in the chairs and the shelves used for the display of glass. The tablecloth is in a chequer pattern overlaid with black ribbon stripes.

The guest bedroom is also lustrous in black and white, this time with walls in a chequer pattern that looks like black lacquer overlaying blemishless white Carrara marble; the white is in fact fabric. There is a black chest of drawers beside the bed with ivory-white round nobs. Built into the bedhead are two picture frames with engravings of a baroque triumphal arch and a temple folly. The pair of stick lamps complement both, with a white section at the top like a candle. Hempel says, 'I use a lot of framed architectural prints. I never skimp. I want them to march around the room.'

The bathroom is equally dashing with mirrors on three sides enlarging its broom-cupboard size – you step into the bath at its short end. The white panels below the bath and the dado are edged in black, perfectly matched by the towels and floor mat.

In the master bedroom there is a parallel play on varied stripes: broad stripes for the bed, narrow ones for the curtains, and then the favourite gondola poles in spiralling black and white ribbon.

The idea for the apartment was sparked by a spectacular Russian Biedermeier desk in mahogany and ebony. Hempel explains, 'I could invent its past. Would it have been made for a black palace, burnished with gold? Could it have been used by a moody Onegin? Perhaps Tatyana swept past it on her way to the ball? Those were the fantasies behind these rooms.'

The master bedroom is a clever play on black and white stripes: narrow, broad and spiralling

ANOUSKA HEMPEL

The living room in tones of black, grey and silver with a play on striped and chequered fabric. Over the fireplace is a portrait of two boys by Giovanni Boldoni, 1890

Opposite: In the dining room lustrous mahogany tempers the leitmotif of cool black and white stripes. The tall ebony panelled doors are inspired by Sir John Soane's Bank of England

In the bathroom, mirrors create the illusion of space with towels and
bathmat echoing the black and white of the walls

Opposite: The guest bedroom is an essay in brilliantly illuminated
contrasting black and white stripes, with matching fabrics for the bed

FROM THE MOMENT YOU SET EYES ON HER PIRATE BLACK SAILS
you know you are in for an adventure. For *Beluga* is a boat unlike any other, as
theatrical, fun and unpredictable as its creator.

When the children were young the Weinbergs chartered a succession of
yachts in the Caribbean and the Mediterranean, latterly spending ever more
time in the sapphire blue waters off the Turkish coast. Determined to have a boat
of her own, Anouska Hempel, with her unerring eye for line, decided the one to
buy was a traditional Turkish gulet. She was told to go to Bodrum at the end of
the season. Arriving in October she found the boats out of the water, held aloft
on stilts in the Turkish manner, so their lines were visible at a glance. 'I bought
her for the lovely shape of her undercarriage, high at the back and tugged down
at the tummy – tightly waisted,' she explains.

Hempel continues, 'I didn't want a horrid white job. This is a more romantic
notion of travel. In a gulet you can be a gypsy on water.' Having struck the bargain,
Hempel was not going to lose a moment. Making straight for the nearest bar, she
found two Turkish sailors and promptly engaged them to sail *Beluga* to Majorca
for a major refit. 'They sailed by the stars. I did it on trust, promising to fly them
back via Izmir to see their grandmothers.' When *Beluga* arrived in Majorca she
looked a tramp. 'There was no question of her going into the marina at Palma.
She had to go to the old harbour in Palma alongside the fishing vessels.'

The refit took two years. The hull and masts were full of woodworm. All the
joinery work was done by Paul Carter who lived on board for nearly a year. Since
initial work was completed, *Beluga* has been through four makeovers, first pale
ginger, then white followed by navy blue, now black and ginger. Steadily she has
become darker and moodier.

'She has never looked better than in these waters,' Sir Mark texted me the
day before I set out. Driving from Dalaman over the crest of coastal hills in
southwest Turkey, we suddenly looked down on a vast blue bay surrounded by
hills and islands covered in pines, which remained as fresh as spring in the full
heat of summer. Not a building was in sight in the entire 48-kilometre circuit of
the bay. *Beluga* had come home.

'Gulets were the summer homes of Turkish families. They'd anchor and lash
the boats together, placing platforms between to form a floating deck,' explains
Hempel. Now, as then, the food market comes to the gulets in dinghies selling
fresh fish and seafood, vegetables and bread.

The striking feature of *Beluga* and the other gulets moored around the bay
is the awnings over the stern, forming a shaded outside sitting and dining area.
Others were white or red, none black like *Beluga*.

Hempel's artistic energies as usual are focused on creating both a look and a
mood. The aft deck has divans over the stern, around 1.8 metres deep and long
enough to sleep on, but stocked with so many navy blue cushions that you can

Beluga is a gulet, the traditional floating
summer home of Turkish families

sit at the table. Once on board, the central gangway to the stern becomes a still grander pasha seat. The table is in two parts, which join up to seat a party of twenty-six when friends moor nearby.

In summer, at this end of the Mediterranean, the need is for cooling shade not sun. Raffia blinds roll down, reducing the view to a shimmering glimpse of sun reflected on the sea. When the wind picks up, a second set of inner blinds is unrolled. *Beluga*'s canopy posts are simple scaffold poles. 'I wrap them round with cane. It's good to grip on,' says Hempel. For a party, she adds big ginger ribbons. In the heat, the cabin doors are permanently folded back, opening up the main cabin to the aft deck. On either side are large cane chairs from a colonial club in Bombay, darkened to make them look smarter.

The secret ingredient of *Beluga*'s furnishings is, as always, shopping. Hempel mixes the smartest and chicest with the cheapest and simplest. 'I love to find things at weekend markets in the back hills of Provence. I call it "lateral looking,"' she says. 'Takashimaya in Fifth Avenue, New York, is my favourite shop in the world. The Japanese people there have a fantastic eye. They tell me where things come from so I can buy more from the source.' The look is strengthened by repetition, by furnishings and objects grouped in pairs, threes and fours. Strict symmetry reigns throughout the main deck. Within the cabin are the trademark trunks in white calfskin and vellum, specked with age and a green patina on the lock plates.

On the trunks, trays are filled with marshalled sets of matching pots and stacks of smart leather underplates with stitched edges and coordinating leather napkin rings. Boxes made of porcupine quills are grouped nearby. When dinner is laid, the table placements are a sculptural display. I counted a pyramid of seven successive plates: tin from Turkey, pewter from Italy, marble from India. The

Glancing light creates shadow patterns, picking up the colour and texture of the cushions and blinds

Beluga's pirate-black sails transform her silhouette when unfurled, here seen both ways against a sunset sky

pewter plate with an ornate Gothic 'W' came from a shop in Tetbury, England. Technology, usually on proud display in a yacht, is all but invisible. Ceiling lights are no larger than old-fashioned pennies, speakers are unseen, light switches barely distinguishable from the panelling.

As we descend below deck, Hempel explains, 'When I bought her there were ten to twelve cabins. It was a tourist nonsense done for Swedish kids sunbathing on deck all day long and living hugger-mugger below.' Now the typical layout of the gulet has been reversed. The crew sleep on stepped bunks in two cabins at the stern with the galley amidships. Hempel continues, 'You have to be very practical and clever using every nook and cranny. A place for everything and everything in its place.'

The numerous practical touches include a wood rim to the Belfast sink to avoid chipping plates. Drawers have no handles so there is nothing to catch on. Large baskets containing plates and kitchen equipment are on tracks so they glide out smoothly despite their weight. Oversize Irish serving spoons have curled handles so they can be hung above the draining board. Kitchen knives and sharpener hang nearby in leather holsters. Despite the confined space the chef can lay out twenty-six plates as food is served. 'We need two ovens and an ice cream machine. We have to shop every second day,' he says.

The main cabins are approached down a short flight of steps by the bridge. The unusual carved emblems on the doors are cheese graters from Thailand.

Dining at anchor *à deux* off black and white porcelain and on folding chairs, which are a precise colour match for the woodwork

Bathroom fittings are edged with smart brass piping. These are sections of gun-cleaning rods bought in a junk shop in Tetbury and cut to fit by Paul Carter.

The mattresses are all from Sleeping Partners. 'They make them up specially soft but firm and sprung within,' explains Hempel. Place mats stand in for prints on the walls. Bedside lamps have conical shades like coolie hats. The roll down blinds are from the Ivory Coast. Towels are stacked or hung in diminishing sizes, four sets in all. Boxes of Acqua di Palma cologne and shampoo are set out in perfect symmetry.

'Maintenance is a non-stop job. In summer you need to protect surfaces from the blistering heat. That's why the boat has a second skin of canvas. You need to rub down every surface every two weeks to protect from salt. Anything exposed to salt water corrodes. The mahogany rail must be constantly wiped down,' continues Hempel.

Beluga came with a Polish tractor engine, which remains. Sir Mark has added auxiliary bow thrusters, which operate like jets and can be used to drive the boat if necessary. The captain explains: 'the water in the bay is very deep. Everyone moors stern-to. We need a chain four times the length of the boat. In 25 metres of water all the chain is out. It's the weight of the chain which acts as a buffer against wind. Ours weighs 700 kilos acting as a huge counterweight.'

Beluga is the perfect boat for gently exploring the unspoilt beauty of Mediterranean bays. Under sail you have sudden tantalizing glimpses of fishing villages in hidden coves, some abandoned since the Greeks left nearly one hundred years ago. When you slip into the water to swim across a small bay, your eye is caught by the entrance of an ancient tomb half hidden amidst the trees. Back on the boat, iced cocktails are waiting. *Beluga* is built for pampering, ensuring you have a heightened sense of the beauty all around you.

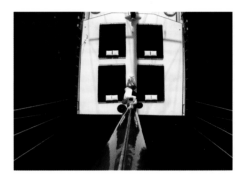

Sunbeds on the cabin roofs form matching pairs

Monogrammed napkins in leather straps sit on crested porcelain on stitched leather plates. Wine glasses are etched with a coat of arms inset with a shield

Place settings for an al fresco lunch beneath the
awnings over the stern, which form a shaded
sitting and dining area. The table is in two parts,
which join up to seat a party when friends
moor nearby

Opposite: Looking out to the pine-clad slopes
around the great bay south of Göcek, studded
with islands and promontories

Above and opposite: In the main cabin the need in summer is for cooling shade not sun. Raffia blinds roll down over the windows. The trademark trunks in white calfskin and vellum are chosen for their patina of age and handsome lock plates

Overleaf: Sunbeds laid out over the stern at sunset. The handrail behind the beds lifts up to provide access to the stern

Above and opposite: Large, generous beds fill the cabins, while clothes are stored in wicker baskets each in its own deep shelf, avoiding the need for cupboard doors that intrude in a small space

Left: A heron in a characteristic one-leg pose adorns a navy blue hanging

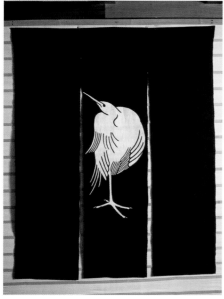

A cabin with a double bed and navy blue trim

Bathroom fittings are edged with
smart brass piping and sections of
gun-cleaning rods

The cabins were moved from the stern to the bow. Place mats on the pillows match the bed-cover and a classic Hempel hat sits in the basket

A selection of porcelain and cutlery provide constantly changing and always pretty table placements

The aft deck balustrade stands open in
welcome of approaching visitors

Overleaf: The gangway closed as *Beluga* glides
across the bay leaving barely a trace of wash

ACKNOWLEDGMENTS

The work of Anouska Hempel has become known the world over thanks to numerous articles in *The World of Interiors*, *House and Garden*, *Homes & Gardens* and *Architectural Digest*, as well as in many leading foreign-language design and interior magazines around the world, including the Italian edition of *AD*, *Elle Decoration*, *Maison* and *Madame Figaro*. Min Hogg and Elizabeth Lambert have written extensively about her work. The photographs for these articles were taken by many renowned photographers, including Tim Beddow, Adrian Houston, Derry Moore, James Mortimer, Durston Saylor, Marianne Haas, Cees Roelofs, George Bamford, Andrew Lawson, Simon Upton, Andrew Denley, Jeremy Hudson, Lord Snowdon and Fritz von der Schulenburg.

For their contributions to this volume, Marcus Binney would like to thank:

Sir Mark and Lady Weinberg; Nancy Cogswell and Paul Morris at Anouska Hempel Design; Belinda Harley; Paul Carter and William Bertram; Marcella Baraldi in Milan; Joy Whitehouse; Dr Michael and Caroline Feichtinger; Imogen Graham for additional picture research; Michael Mitchell and Susan Wightman at Libanus Press; Jamie Camplin and Laura Potter at Thames & Hudson; and my wife Anne for her many thoughtful observations on the text.

For their contributions to Anouska Hempel Design, Lady Weinberg would like to thank:

Sir Mark Weinberg	Russell Jones
Neville Ablitt	Freddy Mauwer
William Bertram	Henny Mauwer
Marcus Binney	Paul Morris
Anthony Brindle	Julie Perrin
Paul Carter	Emma Rayner
Helena Clunies-Ross	Doreen Scott
Martin Evans	Carolynne Shenton
Xavier Fernandes	Manuela da Silva
Sarah Graham	Dave Taylor
Richard Harding	Hugh Tuffley
Belinda Harley	David Vaughan Hughes
Cheryl Howard	

Nicholas d'Archimbaud 102 (top and bottom), 104, 113 (all), 115, 118, 119, 131, 138 George Bamford 9 Henry Bourne 283 Paul Brady 150 (top and bottom) James Brittain 14 (top) Helena Clunies-Ross 234 (bottom) Andreas von Einsiedel 196–209 Marina Faust 8, 12 (top), 14 (bottom left and right), 15 (bottom), 18–19, 27 Justin Gallagher 140 (top and bottom) Sarah Graham 51, 52 Marrianne Haas 12 (bottom), 166 (top and bottom), 268, 269 (all), 274, 275, 278 (top and bottom), 279 Adrian Houston 10 (all), 49, 63 (all), 64–65, 66–67, 68, 70–71, 105 (top), 106, 107, 108, 109 (bottom), 110–11, 112, 114, 122, 133 (all), 134, 135 (all), 136 (all), 137, 139 (top and bottom), 142 (bottom), 143 (bottom right), 210, 211, 212 (top and bottom), 234 (top), 235, 236, 237 (all), 238, 239 (all), 270, 271 (top and middle right), 272, 273, 276–77, 284–85 Menno Landstra 148 (top and bottom), 149 (bottom), 151 (top), 152–53, 154–61 Andrew Lawson 13 (top), 31 (top right and bottom), 73 (top and bottom), 74, 77 (top and bottom), 78–79, 81 (bottom), 84 (all), 85 (top and bottom), 244 (bottom), 245, 246–47, 250, 251 (top and bottom) Massimo Listri 11, 252–61 Simon Mack 141 (top), 144 (bottom) Cameron Maynard 30, 31 (top left), 34–35, 37 (top), 38 (top and bottom), 39 (top and bottom), 41 (all), 43 (right), 45, 48 (all), 52, 54, 55 (top left and bottom), 59, 82 (top), 87 (bottom right), 142 (top), 143 (top and bottom left), 146, 147 (all), 190 (top), 191, 193 (bottom right and left), 195 Paul Morris 13 (bottom), 75 (bottom right), 141 (bottom), 229 (top and bottom right), 271 (bottom), 282 (all) James Mortimer 216–17, 241, 242–43 Clive Nichols 75 (top and bottom left), 76 (bottom right and left), 80 (top and bottom), 86 (top and bottom) Will Pryce 175–187, 188, 189, 190 (bottom), 192, 193 (top), 194 George Ramos 149 (top) Cees Roelofs 82 (bottom), 229 (bottom left) Durston Saylor 262–67 Fritz von der Schulenberg 36, 40, 43 (left), 44, 46, 56 (all), 72, 81 (top), 83 (top and bottom) Nick Scott 172 Simon Upton 6–7, 15 (top), 16, 17 (top and bottom), 28–29, 32, 33, 42 (all), 47, 50, 53 (all), 55 (top and middle right), 57 (all), 58, 60, 61, 62, 69 (all), 105 (bottom), 109 (top left and right), 116, 117, 120, 121 (all), 123, 124–25, 126–27, 128, 129, 132, 168 (top and bottom), 173, 213 (top and bottom), 214, 215 (all), 218, 219 (top and bottom), 220, 221 (all), 222–23, 224, 225, 226, 227, 228, 230–31, 232, 233, 240, 244 (top), 248–49 Joao Vaz Guedes 151 (bottom) Lady Weinberg 144 (top), 145 Jonathan Weinberg 76 (top), 280 (top and bottom), 281 Sir Mark Weinberg 37 (bottom right and left) Arnault Van West 162 (top and bottom), 163 (right and left), 164, 165, 167 (all), 169, 170, 171 Kim Zwarts 88–101

ANOUSKA HEMPEL, LADY WEINBERG, is of Swiss, German and Irish ancestry. She grew up in New Zealand, arriving in London in the mid-1960s after extensive travels. Here, she established herself as a leading designer renowned for her sophistication and style, creating hotels and interiors as well as sensational gardens, clothes and food. Her practice, Anouska Hempel Design, works extensively in the Americas, Europe, Africa, and the Middle and Far East.

MARCUS BINNEY studied History of Art and Architecture at Cambridge. His interest in interiors grew from writing articles for *Country Life*, which were subsequently published as *The Great Houses of Europe* and became a 39-part television series. His other books include *The Ritz Hotel London, In Search of the Perfect House, The Women who Lived for Danger* and *Secret War Heroes*. He is Architecture Correspondent of *The Times* of London.

BELINDA HARLEY has produced acclaimed books on Harry's Bar and Annabel's in London. She has a special interest in the design of hotels and restaurants.